"ANALYSIS OF PROFITABILITY OF SELECTED ELECTRONICS INDUSTRY IN INDIA"

:: Author ::

Labhuben Godhaniya

(M.Com., M.Phil., Ph.D(continue…))

PUBLISHED BY

The New Era International Publishing House
HQ. At & Po. Chaveli., Ta- Chansma,
Dist- Patan, North Gujarat, India, Asia.
www.iphouseindia.com

First Publication: 6th March, 2015

Copyright: Author

(c) **Labhuben Godhaniya**

ISBN:- 978-15-08949-76-3

Price: Rs.750/- INDIA

$ 15 OUTSIDE INDIA

PUBLISHED BY

**The New Era International Publishing House
HQ. At & Po. Chaveli., Ta- Chansma,
Dist- Patan, North Gujarat, India, Asia.
www.iphouseindia.com**

CHAPTER 1

CONCEPTUAL FRAMEWORK OF PROFITABILITY

1 INTRODUCTION

2 CONCEPTS OF 'PROFIT' AND 'PROFITABILITY'

3 FACTORS AFFECTING THE PROFITABILITY

4 SIGNIFICANCE OF PROFITABILITY

5 TECHNIQUES TO MEASURE PROFITABILITY

> 5.1 CONCEPT OF RATIO ANALYSIS
>
> 5.2 PURPOSE AND TYPES OF RATIOS
>
> 5.3 IMPORTANCE OF RATIO ANALYSIS
>
> 5.4 BENEFITS OF RATIO ANALYSIS
>
> 5.5 LIMITATIONS OF RATIO ANALYSIS

1. Introduction:

Business is conducted primarily to earn profits. The amount of profit earned measures the efficiency of a business. The greater the volume of a profit, the higher is efficiency of the concern. The profit of a business may be measured and analyzed by studying the profitability of investments attained by the business.

Profit is the main goal for establishing a business concern. Profit is the primary motivating force for economic activity. Profits have to be earned and they have got to be earned on a regular or continuous basis. Business concerns that is unable to generate sufficient profits from their operations cannot remunerate the providers of their capital and this makes it difficult for them to maintain the continuity of their existence. Profits are needed not only to remunerate capital but also to finance growth and expansion. The survival of a firm in growing economy cannot always be ensured simply by maintaining the status queue. If the firm is to survive in competitive and expanding environment, it has to go on expanding the scale of its operations on a regular and continuing basis. "Profits are the record card of the past, the inventive lord star for the future. If an enterprise fails to make Profit, capital invested is eroded and in this situation prolongs the enterprise ultimately ceases to exist."[1] Thus profit is the soul of the business concern without which it becomes weak and lifeless. In fact profits are useful intermediate beacon towards which a firm's capital should be directed.

2. Concept of 'Profit' and 'Profitability':

❖ Profit

The word 'Profit' has had French / Latin origin in 'Proficere' (being useful or proficient), 'Profectus' and 'Profectum' (to make progress). Thus, profit is in index of proficiency or progress, as typified by 'the gain resulting from the employment of capital', the excess of returns over expenditure; pecuniary gain in any transaction / occupation.

Profit can arise when the price paid by the customers for the product of the business firm exceeds the cost that has been incurred for it. Profit has been defined in a number of ways, by accountants, economists and others as per its use and purpose. There have been many theoretical discussion of the concept of profit, but there is no consensus on the precise definition of this theoretical construct.[2] In short, Profit means excess of income over expenditure in given period of time. Hence, the excess of output over input factors expressed in monetary term represents profit.

❖ Profitability:

The word 'profitability' is composed of two words 'profit' and 'ability'. Therefore, profitability means the profit making ability of the enterprise. According to Gibson and Boyer, Profitability is the ability of the firm to generate earnings. In the words of **Howard and Upton,** "The concept of profitability may be defined as the ability of a given investment to earn a return from its use."[3] Profitability is an indication of the efficiency with which the operations of the enterprise are carried on. Poor operational performance may indicate poor sales and hence poor profits. A lower profitability may arise due to the lack of control over expenses. In accountancy, profitability may be described as a yard-stick of the enterprise performance and indicate public acceptance of the products. It is a relative concept which regulates and controls management policy and decision. In the words of **Weston and Brigham**, "Profitability is the net result of a large number of policies and decisions."[4] The profitability ratios show the combined effects of liquidity, asset management and debt management on operating results.

❖ Profit And Profitability

Profit is essentially an internal measure of new wealth creation. It reflects the excess of earnings over expenses or costs. If the costs are more than earnings, it will mean a loss. Profit is the excess of net sale revenue over the cost of goods sold while profitability is the profit making ability of the business firm showing either steady or increased or decreased state of such ability during a specified time. Profit is an absolute connotation showing absolute figure which alone cannot give an exact idea of changes in efficiency of business firm whereas profitability is a relative concept which gives a clear idea of variation in efficiency. Thus, profit and profitability are two different concepts; however, they are closely related and mutually interdependent, having distinct role in business. Hence, it can be said that profitability is broader concept comparing to the concept of profit. Profitability is the overall measure of efficiency. The income (output) as compared to the capital employed (input) indicates profitability of a firm.

3. Factors Affecting the Profitability:

The following are the two main factors which affects the profitability of a business firm.

(1) The Operational profit Margin.

(2) The Rapidity of Turnover of capital employed.

Profitability is the product of these two factors and, therefore maximum or optimum profits can be earned only by maximizing them. In technical terms, the combination of these two factors is known as the "Triangular Relationship." Its significance exits not only in its use as an analytical tool but also because the profitability ratio can be calculated directly from the specific earnings and investment data. It is also useful in explaining the two forces bearing upon ultimate results and therefore, establishes the area of business operations which must be properly controlled if expected results are to be achieved. It can be shown is an equation form as under:

$$\text{Profitability} = \frac{\text{Sales}}{\text{Operating Assets}} \times \frac{\text{Operating Income}}{\text{sales}} = \frac{\text{Operating Income}}{\text{Operating Assets}}$$

Where "Operating Assets" are used for capital employed and income from utilization of capital employed in the business firm, respectively. The inter-relationship between the above ratios has to be understood with a view to analyzing profitability. The rate of return on investment is the result of the profit margin and turnover of assets in sales. These two components are multiplied for arriving at the profit percentage on investment. Each of these two components is itself an end -product of a sequence of interrelated factors. These components are helpful in investigating the financial composition, analyzing current financial position and formulating the financial forecasting for future of a business firm.

4. Significance of Profitability:

Profit is a very good indicator of business performance, but the real standard of performance of a business firm cannot be judged by the absolute size of its periodic profit. For that profitability is a good device, which represent the earning of a business firm. Modern management is engaged in the task of maximizing the profit and wealth. The efficiency of management is measured by the profitability of the business; the greater is the profitability of the business, the more will be efficiency. An analysis of the profitability reveals as to how the position of profit stands as a result of total transactions made during the year. It need not be stressed that profitability is analyses through the computation of profit ratios. Profitability of a business firm is very much helpful to the management, creditors and shareholders of business firm.

The management of business firm has to take some crucial managerial decision like further expansion, raising of additional finance and problem of bonus and dividend payment etc. and for this purpose the management greatly rely-upon the profitability of the business firm. Moreover, management cans evaluate the operational efficiency of the business firm. The creditors of a business firm are also interested in the profitability of business firm. On the basis of profitability they decide their policy regarding the business firm. The shareholders are equally interested in the profitability of the company. The shareholders of a business firm cannot be judged by absolute size of its periodic profit. For that profitability is a good device which represent the earning capacity of a business firm. Modern management is engaged in the task of maximizing the profits and wealth. The efficiency of management is measured by profitability of the business; the greater is the profitability reveals as to how position of profit stands as a result of total transaction mode during the year. It need not be stressed that profitability is analyzed through the computation of profit ratios. Profitability of a business firm is very much helpful to the management, creditors and share-holders of business firm. The management of a business firm has to take same crucial managerial decision like further expansion, raising of an additional finance and problem of bonus and dividend payments etc. and for this purpose the management greatly rely-upon the profitability of the business firm. Moreover, management can evaluate the operational efficiency of the business firm. The creditors of a business firm are also interested in the profitability of business firm. On the basis of profitability they decide their policy regarding the business firm. The share-holders are equally interested in the profitability of the company. The share-holders can take the decision whether to hold their equity share in the company or not, on the basis of profitability. Thus the management, creditors and owners of the company are equally interested in the profitability of the company.

5. Evaluation Methods:

A study of liquidity, productivity and financial efficiency through profitability is made by using the following tools and techniques.

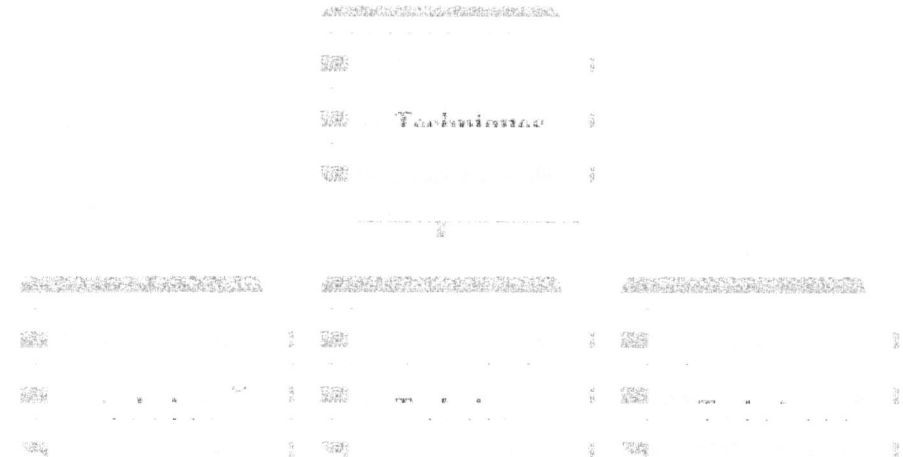

5.1 Accounting Techniques:

Accounting techniques or tool which may use for financial analysis are many such as ratio analysis, common-size statement analysis, trend analysis, comparative statement analysis, Fund flow Analysis, cash flow Analysis, value added analysis etc. The users pick up the techniques to suit their requirements and also on the basis of data available to them.

1. Comparative Financial Statements:

Comparison of financial statements for two or more years is another technique used in analyzing data. Comparative financial statements are statements of financial position of a business so designed as to provide time perspective to the consideration of various elements of financial position embodied in such statements. For this purpose the balance sheet and profit and loss account are prepared in comparative form. Comparative statements may be made to show.

- Absolute data (rupee amount or money value),
- Increase or decrease in absolute value data in terms of money value and
- Increase or decrease in absolute data in term of percentage.

1.   **Comparative Income Statement:**

The comparative income statement gives an idea of the progress of a business over a period of time. The changes in absolute data in money values and percentages can be determined to analyses the profitability of the business.

2.   Comparative Balance Sheet:

The comparative balance sheet analyses is the study of the trend of the same items, group of items and computed items in two or more balance sheet of the same business enterprise an different dates. The changes in periodic balance sheet items reflect the conduct of a business. The changes can be observed by a comparison of the balance sheet at the beginning and at the end of a period and these changes can help in forming an opinion about the progress of an enterprise.

2. Common-Size Financial Statement:

Profitability is an indication of the efficiency with which the operations of the enterprise are carried on. Quantification of profitability or measurement of profitability is needed for taking policy decision under difference circumstances. The profitability can be measured in terms of different components of income statement or balance sheet. The other tools of measurement cannot explain the changes that have taken place from year to year in relation to total assets, total liabilities or total net sales. Common size analysis can make a comparison between different size firms much more meaningful since the numbers are brought to a common base percentage. Common size statement converts financial statement by expressing absolute rupee amount into percentage.

1.   Common Size Income Statement:

Common size income statement can be shown as percentages of sales to show the relation of each item to sales. A significance relationship can be established between the items of income statements and volume of sales. The increase in sales will certainly increase selling expenses and not administrative or financial expenses. In case the volume of sales increases to a considerable extent, administrative and financial expenses may go up. In case the sales are declining the selling expenses should be reduced at once. So, a relationship is established between the sales and other items in income statement and this relationship is helpful in evaluating operational activities and operational efficiency of a concern.

2.   Common Size Balance Sheet:

A statement in which the balance sheet items are expressed as the ratio of each asset to total assets and the ratio of each liability to total liabilities is called common size balance sheet.

3. Trend Analysis:

Trend analysis makes it easy to understand the changes in any item or a group of items over a period of time and to draw conclusion regarding the changes in data. For this purpose, a base year is chosen and the amount of that item relating to the base year is taken equal to one hundred and index numbers are calculated for other years based on the amount of that item in those years. It is a dynamic method of analysis showing the changes over a period of time. For proper trend analysis, the trend should be studied at least over a period of not less than five years. This method of analysis indicates the direction in which a concern is going and upon this basis for future can be made.

❖ **Utility of Trend Analysis:**

This method of analyzing financial statement is more important due to its following merits:

➢ **Summary Presentation:** The problem in this method is presented in a summary from as larger figures are converted into percentage or ratios which are comparatively more useful.

➢ **Direction of Change:** The direction of changes can be even more clearly and easily represented by graphs and bar diagrams.

➢ **Simple Method:** this method of analysis is simple and easy to present. The results obtained can easily be understood by a common man. More trained personnel's are not required as an average person can analyses the data.

➢ **No Possible of Errors**: in this method, the possibility of committing errors is reduced because results obtained from percentage changes in data can be verified from absolute changes.

4. Value Added Analysis:

The concept of value added is considerably old. Value added is the wealth a reporting entity has been able to create through the collective effort of capital, management and employees. Value added is the wealth that a firm creates by its own efforts. Value added statement is the indicator of corporate performance for shareholders and stakeholders who contributes in the process of addition of value to product. The value added statements has several advantages. The value added statement is a good measure of the overall productivity of the firm and it is out of the value added that the firm rewards all interested parties. Value added based ratios are useful diagnostic and predictive tools. Value added statement is very good measure of the size and importance of an enterprise.

5. Fund Flow Analysis:

In financial statements, balance sheet shows assets, liabilities and equity of the firm at a certain moment of time. Profit and loss account depicts operating results over a period of time. Both these financial statements do not depict the flows of funds and changes in the items of assets and liabilities between two dates. Hence, a funds flow of funds and statement is prepared to know the different sources of funds and their different uses. This funds flow statement is a summary report of financial operations of a business enterprise, in which it is explained, how business activities are financed and how the financial resources of the business are being used.

6. Cash Flow Analysis:

In any business, it is essential to known the sources of cash and the items on which it is spent. Funds flow statement does not provide such information, because many items not relating to cash are included in funds flow statement. Therefore, to know about the flows of cash during an accounting period, a separate statement known as cash flow statement is prepared. Thus, cash flow statement is a statement of inflows (sources) and outflows (users) of cash and cash equivalents in an enterprise during a specified period of time. With this statement, the causes for variation in the cash balance between any two dates are interpreted.

7. Cost Volume Profit Analysis:

Cost volume profit analysis is a technique for studying the relationship between cost volume and profit. Profit of an undertaking depend a large number of factors. But the most important of these factors are cost of manufacture, volume of sales and the selling prices of the products. The CVP relationship is an important tool used for the profit planning of a business. The CVP relationship is of immense utility to management as it assets in profit planning, cost control and decision making.

8. Ratio Analysis:

Analysis of financial statement based on ratios is known as ratio analysis. Ratio analysis is a technique of presenting internal and external events affecting the business transaction relating to its operations, operating results and achievement of pre-determined goals and objectives of a business in brief and summary form. According to **Belverd-E-Needless** "Ratio guides or short cuts that are useful in evaluating the financial position and operations of a company and in comparing them with previous years or with other companies. The primary purpose of ratio is to point out areas for further investigations. They should be used in connection with a general understanding of the company and its environment."[15] In short ratio analysis is the process of determining and presenting is the relationship of items or group of items in the financial statement.

8.1 Concept of Ratio Analysis:

According to **J. Batty** "The term accounting ratio is used to describe significant relationships which exist between figures shown in a balance-sheet, in a profit and loss account, in a budgetary control system or in any other part of the accounting organization." The accounting ratios indicate a quantitative relationship which is used for analysis and decision making. It provides basis for inter-firm as well as intra-firm compression. The ratios will be effective only when they are compared with ratios of base period of with standards or with the industry ratios.

The financial statements viz. income statement and balance sheet report what has actually happened.

"Analysis of an enterprise by financial ratios enables the financial manager as well as interested external parties, to evaluate the firm's financial performance and condition rapidly by making comparisons of ratios obtained from the firm with ratios obtained from other comparable firms." In the words of **Helfert**, "Ratio analysis provides guides and clues especially in spotting trends towards better or poor performance, and in finding out significant deviation from any average or relatively applicable standard." Thus, ratio analysis enables the user to better understand financial statements than by looking at the absolute quantities alone.

According to **Parkinson,** "Ratio which are generally used are grouped in four convenient areas-those concerning the liquidity of the business, its ability to pay the bills when they fall due; the ratios relating to the performance and including the profitability ratios, the ratios on the structure as this has a bearing on the security of loan and the availability of finance, and lastly the financial ratios which look at performance and structure from the view point of the investor and the financial markets."

Industrial sickness in India is ram-pant. One possible reason for industrial sickness is the poor management of liquidity. A firm in order to remain in existence and sustain its activities as a going concern must remain liquid and meet its obligations as and when they become due. A classification system of the functions of financial management links the twin goals of liquidity and profitability. The functions are directed towards achieving either or both of these goals.

8.2 Ratios can be expressed in two ways:

1. Times

When one value is divided by another, the unit used to express the quotient is termed as "Times". For example if out of 100 students in a class, 80 are present; the attendance ratio can be expressed as follows:

$$\frac{80}{100} = 0.8 \text{ times}$$

2. Percentage

If the quotient obtained is multiplied by 100, the unit of expression is termed as "percentage". For instance, in the above example the attendance ratio as a percentage of the total number of students is as follows:

$$= 0.8 \text{ x } 100 = 80\%$$

Accounting ratios are, therefore, mathematical relationships expressed between inter-connected accounting figures.

8.3 Purpose and Types of Ratios:

A ratio form an integral part of the financial statement analysis and is used to measure the various aspects of a business. Financial ratios can be categorized according to the business' financial aspect which is being measured by the ratio.

The Different Types of Ratios:

1. Liquid Ratios:

Short-term creditors are primarily interested in liquidity or short-term solvency of the enterprise since their claims are to be met in the short-run. Liquidity or short-term solvency means the ability of the enterprise to meet short-term obligations as and when they become due. Inability to pay off short-term liabilities affects the credibility of the enterprise. Continuous default on part of the enterprise leads to commercial bankruptcy which may lead to its sickness and dissolution.

2. Solvency Ratios:

Long-term creditors are primarily interested in long-term solvency of the enterprise since their claims are to be met in the long-run. Long-term creditors are the liabilities having maturity after one year. Long-term solvency means the ability of the enterprise to meet long-term obligations on the due date. Long-term lender of funds is basically interested in two things:

a. Safety of principal which is given by way of a loan during the term of the loan.

b. Regular servicing of the loan in the form of payment of interest on loan and repayment of installment of loan.

3. Activity or Efficiency Ratios:

Activity ratios measure the effectiveness with which a firm uses its available resources. These ratios help in commenting on the efficiency of the enterprise in managing its assets. These ratios are also called 'Turnover Ratios' since they indicates the speed with which the resources are being turned or converted into sales or cost of sales.

4. Profitability ratios:

These ratios measure management's overall effectiveness as shown by the return generated on sales and investment. Usually three types of profitability ratios are calculated.

a. In relation to Sales

b. In relation to Investments

c. In relation to Equity Shareholders' funds

The Main Purposes Served by Ratios Include Allowing for Comparisons

- ❖ between industries
- ❖ between companies
- ❖ between various time periods for companies
- ❖ between one company and its industry average

It should be noted that usually ratios hold no meaning if they are not benchmarked against a standard, such as past performance or the performance of another company. Therefore, the ratios of firms in each industry, experiencing different risks, competitions, and capital requirements are generally difficult to be compared.

8.4 Importance of Ratio Analysis:

Ratios are guides or shortcuts that are useful in evaluating the financial position of a company and the operations of a company from scientific facts. It helps in comparison of changes in static data from previous years to current year and with the comparison of other companies as well. In accounting and financial management ratios are regarded as the real test of earning capacity, financial soundness and operating efficiency of business concern.

➢ **Simplifies Accounting Figures:**

The most significant objective of ratio analysis is that it simplifies the accounting figures in much easier way by which anyone can be understood it quite easily even for those who do not know the language of accounting.

➢ **Measures Liquidity Position:**

Liquidity position of a firm is said to be satisfactory if it is able to meet its current obligation as and when they mature. A firm is said to be capable of meeting its current obligation only, if it has sufficient liquid funds to pay its short- term obligations within a period of year. Hence, the liquidity ratios are used for the purpose of credit analysis by banks and other short-term lenders.

➤ Measures Long-term Solvency:

Ratio analysis is equally important in evaluating the long- term solvency of the firm. It is measured by capital structure or leverage ratios. These ratios are helpful to long-term creditors, security analysts and present and prospective investors, as they reveal the financial soundness or weakness of the firm.

➤ Measures operational Efficiency:

Ratios are useful tools in the hands of management to evaluate the firm's performance over a period of time by comparing the present ratios with the past ratios. Various activity or turnover ratios measure the operational efficiency of the firm. These ratios are used in general by the bankers, investors and other suppliers of credit.

➤ Measures Profitability:

The management as well as owners of a firm is primarily concerned with the overall profitability of the firm. Profit and loss account reveals the profit earned or loss incurring during a period, but fails to convey the capacity of the firm to earn in terms of money of sales. Profitability ratios help to analysis earning capacity of the firm.

Return on investment, return on capital employed, net profit ratios etc. are the best measures of profitability.

> ## Facilities Inter-firm and Intra-firm comparisons:

Ratio analysis is the basic form of comparing the efficiency of various firms in the industry and various divisions of a firm. Absolute figures are not suitable for this purpose, but according ratios are the best tools for inter firm and inter firm comparison.

> ## Trend Analysis:

Trend analysis of ratios reveals whether financial position of the firm is improving or deteriorating over years because it enables a firm to take the time dimension into account. With the help of such analysis one can ascertain whether the trend may be increasing.

8.5 Benefits of Ratio Analysis:

The ratio analysis forms an essential part of the financial analysis which is a vital part of business planning. The key benefits of ratio analysis include:

> ## Determines profitability

Ratio analysis assists managers to work out the production of the company by figuring the profitability ratios. Also, the management can evaluate their revenues to check if their productivity. Thus, probability ratios are helpful to the company in appraising its performance based on current earning.

> ## Helpful in evaluating solvency

By computing the solvency ratio, the companies are able to keep an eye on the correlation between the assets and the liabilities. If, in any case, the liabilities exceed the assets, the company is able to know its financial position. This is helpful in case they wish to set up a plan for loan repayment.

> ## Better financial analysis

Ratio analysis is also helpful to recluses, in addition to shareholders, debenture holders, and creditors. Besides, bankers are also able to know the profitability of the company to find out whether they are able to pay the dividend and interests under a specific period.

> ## Performance analysis

Ratio analysis is also helpful in analyzing the performance of a company. Through financial analysis, companies can review their performance in the past years. This is also helpful in identifying their weaknesses and improving on them.

> ## Forecasting

At present, many companies use ratio analysis to reveal the trends in production. This provides them an opportunity for estimation of future trends and thus the foundation for budget planning so as to determine the course of action for the growth and development of the business.

8.6 Limitations of Ratio Analysis:

Ratio analysis suffers from a number of draw backs. Difficulty in comparison due to....

➢ Ratios are calculated from financial statements which are affected by the financial bases and policies adopted on such matters as depreciation and the valuation of stocks.

➢ Financial statements do not represent a complete picture of the business, but merely a collection of facts which can be expressed in monetary terms. These may not refer to other factors which affect performance.

➢ Over use of ratios as controls on managers could be dangerous, in that management might concentrate more on simply improving the ratio than on dealing with the significant issues. For example, the return on capital employed can be improved by reducing assets rather than increasing profits.

➢ A ratio is a comparison of two figures, a numerator and a denominator. In comparing ratios it may be difficult to determine whether differences are due to changes in the numerator, or in the denominator or in both.

➢ Ratios are inter-connected. They should not be treated in isolation. The effective use of ratios, therefore, depends on being aware of all these limitations and ensuring that, following comparative analysis, they are used as a trigger point for investigation and corrective action rather than being treated as meaningful in them.

➤ The analysis of ratios clarifies trends and weakness in performance as a guide to action as long as proper comparisons are made and the reasons for adverse trends or deviations from the norm are investigated thoroughly.

5.2 Statistical Techniques:

Use of statistical techniques has become a normal phenomenon in any type of analysis. There are various statistical techniques have been used in the financial analysis like Average/Mean, Standard Deviation , Index Numbers ,Correlation and Regression Analysis, Analysis of Time Series, T-Test, F-Test, χ^2- Test or Chi-Square Test.

5.3 Mathematical Techniques:

Financial analysis also involves the use of certain mathematical tools such as Programme Evaluation and Review Techniques (PERT), Critical Path Method (CPM) and Linear Programming etc. However, they are not useful for the present study.

CHAPTER 2
OVERVIEW OF ELECTRONICS INDUSTRY:

1. Introduction

2. Brief History of Electronics Industry

3. Classification of Electronics Industry

4. Globle Electronics Production Scenario

5. Intermediate Goods Importers & Exporters in the Electronics Industry

6. Globle Value Chains In the Electronics Industry

7. Electronics Industry in India

8. Indian Electronics Industry Current Scenario

9. The Electronics Component Industry

10. Growth of Indian Electronics Components Industry

11. Indian Electronics Component Market

12. Overview of the Electronics Components Manufactured In India

13. Changing Trend in the Electronics Component Industry

14. Electronics Production Scenario in India

15. Sector-Wise Exports of Electronics Items

16. Classification of Electronics Industry Production Scenario

1. Introduction:

The Electronics Industry in India took off around 1965 with an orientation towards space and defense technologies. This was rigidly controlled and initiated by the government. This was followed by developments in consumer electronics mainly with transistor radios, Black & White TV, Calculators and other audio products. Colour Televisions soon followed. In 1982-a significant year in the history of television in India - the government allowed thousands of colour TV sets to be imported into the country to coincide with the broadcast of Asian Games in New Delhi. 1985 saw the advent of Computers and Telephone exchanges, which were succeeded by Digital Exchanges in 1988. The period between 1984 and 1990 was the golden period for electronics during which the industry witnessed continuous and rapid growth.

Electronics characterized as continuously changing technology global in nature. Production methods, market opportunities, distribution channels, service resources and competitive pressure, these highlights influence various sectors of economy as well as human life. According to

Cherunilam Francis "Electronics is one the most dynamic industry. Indeed the progress and efficiency of an economy depends to a large extent on application of electronics. The scopes for application of electronics advantages there form are enormous in a modem society. Electronics is indeed a pace setter."

Electronics is significantly influenced the cost structure as well as the quality and productivity standards of most other industry. The main features of the electronics industry are (1) Relatively pollution free (2) Knowledge incentive (3) Rapidly declining cost (4) investment for balanced regional development in the country and (5) global reach. In the Indian context N. Vittal remarked "Electronics industry has witnessed significant growth during the sixth and seventh plan period with the growth rates being 25 and 35 percent respectively".

While according to Ahuja Shobha "The electronics industry, an account of its capability to affect high value addition and create employment opportunities, has emerged as an important industry of our country".

2. Brief History:

The beginning of electronics was laid by physicists back in the 18th and 19th centuries. A big impetus was given by the electronics theory of conduction of metallic. It developed by many outstanding scientists in the late 19th and early 20th century.

The word "Electronics" is derived from "Electron Mechanics", which means the study of the behavior of an electron under different conditions of externally applied fields. Electronics is defined as "That field of science and engineering which deals with electron devices and their utilization". Here, an electron device is a device I which conduction takes place by the movement of electrons, through a Vacuum, a Gas, or a semi-Conductor.

In 1887 was Heinrich Rudolf Hertz (1857-1894) of Germany Famous for his experiments on electromagnetic waves. He was discovered the photo electric effect next year 1888. Alexander Stoletov was Russia. Investigated Hertz discovery and formulated the law of the photo electric effect. The same year Vladimir Ulyanin of Russia built the first selenium photo cells.

Electronics circuit entered a period of rapid evolution with the developments of vacuum tube dsode by Sir John A. Fleming of Britain in 1904. Followed by the discovery of a crystal detector by Pickard in 1906. The same year Dr. Lee De Forest introduced Audi on Tube that could amplify electric signals. Later the vacuum tube triode invented by De Forest in 1907.

B. Rosing of Russia proposed to use a Cathode Ray Tube for image reception and later proved the viability of his invention in the same year.

In the primary era of electronics (1887-1900) business concern with mainly Radio Communication and Telegraph Companies. It shown mainly in American and Britain but after new invention of wireless telegraphy by G. Marcony in 1897 the electronics scenario was enlarged rather than before in the primary stage of Telegraphy. Morse and Merse Key are used for communication. Morse code is consisting of dots and dashes.

"The average speed of wireless telegraphic communication is probably about 20 wpm." However with electronics keyer, good conditions. G. Marcony has a both of talents scientific as well as business and therefore. He established "Wireless Telegraph and Signal Company" at the age of 23 years. After some time the firm name changed as "Marcony Wireless Telegraphic Company". And for the expansion of the company first issue of share capital was 1,00,000 pounds offered that event put good remarks for the electronics industry.

In 1909 H.V. Kovalenkov of Russia built triodes, adapted to service in long distance telephone repeaters.

In 1913 Alexander Missner of Germany (born in Vienna) was the first to use a Vacuum triode as a self-excited vacuum tube signal generator involving feedback. It was derived to decisive influence on the progress of Radio Engineering. Between 1920 and 1930 much of work in the field of electron devices was made. A Hull of USA made for reaching improvements in the screen grod tetrode and in the year 1930 he took out a patent on the pentode which is as already noted the most extensively used of all types of vacuum tubes.

In 1930-31 A. P. Konstantinov and S. I. Kotayev of USSR working independently of each other and as an outcome "Came up with the idea of Television pick up Camera tubes."

While in the USA Vladimir K. Zworykin engaged in research of photo electric emission and Television. These studies lead to his conception of a new type of Television pick up tube, the iconoscope. Which he developed into for a suitable for practical picture transmission? In the 1940's Germanium and silicon diodes, semi-conductors, themoresisters and photo resisters were commercialized in USSR Modern solid state physics "Driven from their crystalline Garden of Eden by the invention of the Transistor in 1948, where the need for theorists became acute." First point contact Transistor was officially announced by V. Bardeen and W. H. Brattain of USA "The invention of Transistor lead to favorable revolution in electronics industry in the world. Transistors opened the flood gate to further developments in electronics." Within almost 10 years of its discovery the process of miniaturization electronic equipment's. First integrated Circuits (ICs) appeared in the market during the early sixties and use of valves nearly became obsolete. Till 1980 the famous Moor's Law that "The component density on chip will double every years."

Was almost followed at present, component density is almost doubling every four years. Due to the rapid developments in integrated circuits Technology starting from the Small Scale Integration 1-30 Gates, Medium Scale Integration 30-300 Gates, Large Scale Integration 300-10(4) Gates, Very Large Scale Integration 10(4) Gates and beyond and with most Ultra Large Scale Integration beyond 10(9) Gates, even the use of individual transistors is becoming unnecessary.

Technological developments in electronics are international in nature and influence various sectors of economies of Nations as well as Human life, Cost structure, Quality and Productivity standards. Information Technology gets thrust from the mixture of communication, computers and entertainment areas. Development in the design and production of silicon chips permitted "Low cost, high speed and versatile information processing, control and storage capacity." Future developments in electronics sector may significantly change the lifecycle.

The current main features of electronics industry are….

1. High value addition due to high skills involved
2. Capital Intensity
3. Multi-disciplinary nature
4. Global Reach
5. High expenditure on R & D
6. Guarded Technologies last two decades putting remarks in the field of electronics and it has change the world scenario by means

of Communication, Mass Media, and Entertainment through electronics area become global.

3. Classification of Electronics Industry:

Electronic Industry classified into major two areas. (1) Equipment Area, (2) Component Area. Electronic equipment industry generally classified five distinct areas. Those are given in bellows.

1. Consumer: Mainly relating to Audio and Video entertainment sector.

2. Industrial: Process Control, Test and Measurement, Medical Instruments.

3. Computers: Digital and Analog Computers, Office Equipments.

4. Communication: (A) Line Communication: Telegraphy, Telex and Broadcast Telephone. (B) Wireless Communication: Satellite Communication, Radar, Facsimile, Radio & Television Broadcasting.

5. Strategic: For Technology Development.

6. Electronic Components: Electro - Mechanical component

1. Consumer Electronics:

Consumer electronics called as the engine for growth of the electronic industry. Because of new major developments in technology and products will share the spotlight for consumer electronics. "It includes Digital Audio, both Digital Compact Cassette and Mini Disc, Radio Broadcast Data System, Home theater, Multimedia, CD Rom, Home

Office/Portable Office, Personal Electronics and Cellular Telecommunications".

2. Industrial Electronics:

Usages of Automatic Control System in industries are increasing day by day. "For Justification of thickness, quality, weight and moisture content of material, smoke detector, power system, and safety devices are applications of industrial electronics".

While medical sciences findings new uses for electronic systems in Preventive, Diagnostic, Bio-analytical, Therapeutic, Research and Education some of the instruments which have been use are:

➤ X-Ray machines for taking pictures of internal bone structure.

➤ Electrocardiogram (ECG) to find the condition of the heart.

➤ Short wave diatheraphy for hearing sprains.

➤ Oscillograph for studying muscle action.

The use of electronics in medical science has expanded so enormously as to start a new branch of study called "Bio Electronics".

Table No. 1

Brief History of Instrumentation and Process Control Equipment's

Sr. no	Year	Product
1	1900-08	Manual Control with Gauges and Valves.

2	1910-20	Large Case instruments in the field.
3	1938-40	Pneumatic Signal & Instruments.
4	1950's	Electronics Signal & Instruments.
5	1952	First Commercial Magnetic Flow meter.
6	1960's	Computers start to be used.
7	1970	PLC's arrive on scene.
8	1975-80	Distributed Control is introduced.
9	1982	A1 (Fuzzy logic/Self tuning etc.)
10	1983	Smart Transmitter introduced
11	1984-85	High Speed Communication.
12	1985	Software for IBM PC coupled to Panel Mounted Controllers.
13	1987	Unix Operating System, Multi Bus.
14	1990	Windows 3.0 and X-Windows.
15	1992	Intelligent I/O.
16	1995	Windows NT 3.5 And 95.

Source: Noel. J. W. "The future Direction of Instrumentations", IED, Mumbai, January 1997, p. 22

3. Computers Electronics:

"The computers industry has growth both in terms of physical output as well as range of products introducing in the market. A wide manufacturing base consisting of Micro, Mini and Super mini mainframe computer including engineering work stations counted." Presently computers play key role for the development of the country with high degree accuracy, motion and counting.

4. Communication and Broadcast:

The progress of country depends upon the availability of economical and rapid means of communication. In the early of 20th century the main application of electronics was in the field of Technology and Telephony that utilize a pairs of wires. However it is now possible.

"Through satellite technology, it provides several new opportunities for information and communication needs. These can be broadly classified as remote sensing, communications and positioning." Although, fiber optic also very useful in the high-speed data communication. "Fiber optic and optical communications provide good examples of systems which incorporate a wide range of devices including those based on semiconductors and those based on the behavior of light in crystals subject to external fields." While Radio and Television broadcasting provide in a means of both communication as well as entertainment.

5. Strategic Electronics:

New industrial policy and department of electronics act as a familiar for strategic electronics and promote growth. "It includes different types of communication antennas in VHF, UHF, L. Bands, and Design review documents for Radar, System design for Target Project etc."

Component electronics has distinct advantages. There are various types of components i.e. active, passive, electro, mechanicals, opto electronics. The growth of components sector depends on the developments in components technology specially the semiconductor devices. The key driving technologies in the electronics sector are 25 Surface Mount Devices and Assembly Technology.

➤ Signal Processing

➤ Micro Electronics

➤ Opto Electronics

➤ Display Technologies

➤ Networks & Software

6. Electronic Components:

The Indian electronics component market is dominated by Electro - Mechanical components like Printed Circuit Boards, Connectors, etc. with about 27% share while Passive components like wound components, resistors, etc. account for about 20% share. Active Components like Integrated circuits, diodes, transistors, picture tubes, etc. constituted for about 24% and 29% share of the component respectively. While the industry composition is not predicated to change substantially, there is a rapid decline in products, such as Cathode Ray Picture Tubes and CD/DVD's which had till recently constituted a significant share of the manufacturing base and market. This is an outcome of advancing technology and consumer preferences.

4. Global Electronics Production Scenario:

Electronics accounts for an important percentage of national GDP with represents a growing proportion of world's production. In early 1920's annual production of Radio's and Phonograms about 20 million dollars while in 1995 reached figure of 856 billion dollars and early 2008 annual production 11,35,548 million euro's and 2013 annual production 12,98,226. It shows progress report of electronics dominance over the world. Table gives the details of production, market shares of electronics world scenario.

Table No. 2

World Electronics Production / Markets (Million Euros)

Country	Production			Market		
	2008	2013	Annual Growth Rate	2008	2013	Annual Growth Rate

			(2008-2013)			(2008-2013)
Europe	251124	246724	-0.4%	241229	260489	1.5%
North America	204317	184900	-2.0%	210349	217986	0.7%
Japan	162760	163970	0.1%	90419	105399	3.1%
China	296607	416070	7.0%	78821	110244	6.9%
Other Asia-pacific	184383	244075	5.8%	81192	114248	7.1%
Rest of the World	36356	42487	3.2%	73347	90207	4.2%
Total World	1135548	1298226	2.7%	1135548	1298226	2.7%

Source: Global Electronics Industry 2010 – 13

The Global electronics production and market as a macro level shows in the table no. 2. It can be seen that the share of production increased of

Europe -0.4 % in 2008 to 1.5% in 2013, North America -2.0% in 2008 to 0.7% in 2013, Japan 0.1% in 2008 to 3.1%in 2013, Asia 5.8% in 2008 to 7.1% in 2013, others 3.2% in 2008 to 4.2% in 2013. While China share of production decreased 7.0% in 2008 to 6.9% in 2013.

Table No. 3

Growth rates for the global electronics industry by Region

Country	2010	2011	2012	2013
Asia	11%	8%	7%	7%
Europe	7%	2%	1%	3%
America	9%	5%	5%	6%
Australia, Newzealand, South Africa	4%	3%	5%	6%
World Total	9%	6%	5%	6%

Source: Global Electronics Industry 2010 - 13

The production Growth rate in Major Countries during the period 2010 to 2013 is shows in table no. 3. All countries are having slow growth mainly. Asia country was growth rate continually decreasing, growth rate it was 11% in 2010, 8% in 2011and 7% in 2012 and 2013. Europe country continually decreasing growth rate it was 7% in 2010, 2% in 2011, and 1% in 2012 and then after increasing growth rate it was 3% in

2013. America country decreasing growth rate it was 9% in 2010, 5% in 2011 and 2012 and then after increasing growth rate it was 5% in 2013. Australia, Newzealand, South Africa country decreasing growth rate it was 4% in 2010, 3% in 2011 and then after increasing growth rate it was 5% in 2012 and 6% in 2013. Last World total decreasing growth rate it was 9% in 2010, 6% in 2011, 5% in 2012 and increasing growth rate it was 6% in 2013.

5. Intermediate Goods Importers and Exporters in the Electronics Industry:

In the past 20 years, East Asia in general and China in particular have become increasingly important in electronics as well as other industries, both as production locations and final markets. This is reflected in the flow of intermediate goods. Table no. 4 shows, "greater China" (Mainland China, Hong Kong, and Taiwan) accounts for 33.1 percent of world imports of intermediate electronics goods and 29.4 percent of exports. Growth since 1988, especially on mainland China, has been extraordinarily high. The tendency for trade to be intra-industry, that is, for countries to specialize in imports and exports in the same industry, is also striking. All 15 countries in table no. 4 appear on both the top importer and exporter lists, albeit in slightly different rank order after the top four: China, Hong Kong, the United States, and Singapore. While strong intra-industry trade can be a function of transshipment (for example, importing and exporting materials and parts via Hong Kong and perhaps Singapore), the tendency for specific countries to both import and export intermediate products in the same industry reveals the highly integrated nature of the global economy and, for developing countries, the rich opportunities for industrial upgrading, even when parts imports are high.

Table No. 4

Top-15 Intermediate Goods Importers and Exporters in the Electronics Industry, 2006

Electronics Intermediate Imports	US$ millions	% of Total	% Change 1988-2006	Electronics Inermediate Exporters	US$ millions	% of Total	% Change 1991-2006
China	1,86,294	18.9	15219	China	109,433	11.7	21,649.10
Hong Kong	104,856	10.6	1452.2	Hong Kong	101,873	10.9	25800
United States	94,466	9.6	194	United States	101,807	10.9	1794
Singapore	73,040	7.4	590.5	Singapore	97,278	10.4	942.2
Germany	51,569	5.2	236.3	Japan	88,994	9.5	160.8
Japan	45,639	4.6	422.5	Taiwan	63824	6.8	834
Malaysia	44,695	4.5	466.8	Korea	55028	5.9	543.2
Taiwan	35,899	3.6	405.6	Germany	52685	5.7	235.5
Mexico	35,705	3.6	3048.9	Malaysia	43966	4.7	512.9
Korea	35,486	3.6	365.8	Netherlands	30637	3.3	520.2
Netherlands	26,868	2.7	392.9	United Kingdom	22538	2.4	121.1

Philippines	23,685	2.4	1052.6	Philippines	22024	2.4	1186.4
United Kingdom	23,130	2.3	79.5	France	19148	2.1	131.3
France	19,577	2	118.8	Thailand	15756	1.7	438.6
Thailand	18,607	1.9	423.3	Mexico	13115	1.4	3594.1

Source: Global Value Chains in the Electronics Industry, the World Bank September 2010

6. Global Value Chains in the Electronics Industry:

As the nationalities of the well-known firms listed in Table no. 5 suggest, most important lead firms in the electronics industry are based in industrialized countries, especially the United States, Western Europe, and Japan. Of newly industrialized countries, Republic of Korea (hereafter, "Korea") stands out as a base of important lead firms, especially Samsung and LG. Because of their role as production platforms and contract manufacturing centers, only a handful of important lead firms have emerged from developing countries, including Acer, a PC company based in Taiwan; Huawei, a Chinese manufacturer of networking equipment; and Lenovo, a Chinese PC company that leapt onto the world stage with the acquisition of IBM's PC division in 2004. Later in the paper we discuss the possibility that lead firms from developing countries are finding new ways to compete successfully in global markets, and that the recent economic crisis has provided lead firms based in Taiwan with new opportunities to move into more important roles as lead firms in the electronics industry.

Table No. 5

Main Electronics Markets, Products, and Lead Firms

Main Market Segments	Product Examples	Lead Firm Examples
1. Computers	Enterprise computing systems, PCs (desktop, notebook, net book), embedded computers	IBM, Fujitsu, Siemens, Hewlett-Packard, Dell, Apple, Acer, Lenovo
2. Computer peripherals and other office equipment	Printers, fax machines, copiers, scanners	Hewlett-Packard, Xerox, Epson, Kodak, Cannon, Lexmark, Acer, Fujitsu, Sharp
3. Consumer electronics	Game consoles, television, home audio and video, portable audio and video, mobile phone handsets, musical equipment, toys	Toshiba, NEC, Vizio, Sony, Sharp Apple, Nintendo, Microsoft, Samsung, LG, NEC, Matsushita, Hitachi, Microsoft, HTC, Philips
	Portable, internal,	Toshiba, Western

4. Server and storage Devices	external, backup systems, storage services	Digital, EMC, NetApp, Hewlett-Packard, Hitachi, Seagate, Maxtor, LeCie, Quantum
5. Networking	Public telecommunications, private communications networks, Internet, mobile phone infrastructure	Alcatel, Nortel, Cisco, Motorola, Juniper, Huawei, Ericsson, Nokia, Tellabs
6. Automotive Electronics	Entertainment, communication, vehicle control (braking, acceleration, traction, suspension), vehicle navigation	TomTom, Garmin, Clarion, Toyota, General Motors, Renault, Bosch, Siemens
7. Medical electronics	Consumer medical, diagnostics and testing, imaging, telemedicine, meters and monitoring, implants, fitness	General Electric, Philips, Medtronic, Varian

8. Industrial electronics	Security and surveillance, factory automation, building automation, military systems, aircraft, aerospace, banking and ATM, transportation	Diebold, Siemens, Rockwell, Philips, Omron, Dover
9. Military and aerospace electronics	Ground combat systems, aircraft, sea based systems, eavesdropping and surveillance, satellites, missile guidance & intercept	L-3 Communications, Lockheed Martin, Boeing, BAE Systems, Northrop Grumman, General Dynamics, EADS, L-3 Communications, Finmeccanica, United Technologies

Source: Global Value Chains in the Electronics Industry, the World Bank September   2010

7. Electronics Industry in India:

The Indian electronic industry has been in the forefront of the Indian manufacturing revolution. While the industry dates back to the mid-1960s, its progress slowed down considerably in the 1990's due to intense international competition, lowering of customs duties and lack of a supportive eco-system which did not provide it a level playing field. More recently the industry has witnessed higher growth due to consistent and high rate of market growth as well as several government policy changes to encourage manufacturing by ironing out the anomalies in the tax system. The development of the Indian electronic industry can be grouped in to four major time periods in which the industry took shape. They are as follows:

The *"Dawn"* (1960- 1980):- The electronic industry in India dates back to the early 1960s. It was initially restricted to the development and maintenance of fundamental communications systems including radio-broadcasting, telephony, telegraphic communication & augmentation of defense capabilities. This was rigidly controlled and investments were largely initiated by the government.

The *"Golden"* Era (1980-1991):- Until 1984, the electronics sector was primarily government owned. The late 1980's witnessed a rapid growth of the electronic industry with products like transistor radios, Black & White TV, Calculator and other audio products entering the Indian market. In 1982 – a significant year in the history of television in India – the government allowed thousands of color TV sets to be imported into the country to coincide with the broadcast of Asian Games in New Delhi. The year 1985 saw the advent of computers and telephones exchanges, which were succeeded by Digital Exchanges in 1988. The period between 1984 & 1990 was the golden period for the electronics industry during which the sector witnessed continuous and rapid growth.

Era of "*Reckoning*" (1991-2002):- In 1991, the government opened the country's doors to the world and allowed private investments – both domestic and foreign in many of the industries. The easing of the foreign investment norms, allowing 100 percent foreign equity, reduction in custom tariff and de-licensing of several consumer electronics products attracted significant amount of foreign collaboration and investment. The domestic market also responded favorably to the prudent polices of the government. The opening of electronics industry to private sector enabled entrepreneurs to establish industries to meet hitherto suppressed demand.

Era of "*Pursuit*" (2002 onwards):- The investments triggered by the liberalization process was not limited to one sector but encompassed all sectors like consumer electronics, telecommunications, instrumentation, positioning & networking systems, and defense. This period saw both Multinational and Domestic companies establish manufacturing units in India.

India signed the ITA-1 (Information Technology Agreement) in 1997 which was implemented in 2005. The ITA-1 under the WTO is solely a tariff cutting mechanism as per which the duties for all ICT products and their inputs (217 Tariff Lines) are to be abolished allowing for import at zero duty into the signatory countries. The implementation of ITA-1 propelled the growth of Multinational companies in India who were keen to access the growing market. However this also resulted in serious challenges to domestic manufacturing which was not able to compete with global companies due to higher cost structures in the Indian economy.

The implementation of ITA also led to government making amendments in the EXIM policy 2002-2007 to simplify the existing import-export procedure especially for imports to help reduce the price difference between the Indigenous manufacturers and imports. The changes in policies initiated by the government helped the market to grow at a brisk pace of about 25% per annum.

8. Indian Electronic Industry Current Scenario:

During the past five years the electronics industry in India has been driven mainly by Telecom products including equipment and mobile phones, IT Products & components and consumer electronics & durables sector. The growth in demand for telecom products & consumer durables has been breathtaking and is expected to continue over the next decade. Table no. 6 show the demand growth of the key product segments which drive the demand for electronic components.

Table No. 6

Indian Electronic Industry- Current Scenario

Segments	Million Units Sold in				
	2007-08	2008-09	2009-20	2010-11	2011-12
Mobile Phones	96	103	108	138.6	177.82
CRT Television	15	13.97	15.15	15.7	16.27
LCD Television	-	2.7	3.3	6.6	9.7
MP3 Players	4.69	5.45	6.32	7.33	8.5
Set Top Boxes	3	5	7.5	10	13.3
Washing Machines	2.29	2.62	3.35	4.21	5.27
Passenger Cars	1.55	1.55	1.95	2.42	3
2 Wheelers	7.25	7.44	9.37	11.79	14.83

Source: ELCINA, Dept. of IT Ministry of Communication & IT Govt. of India

The above table no. 6 shows the Indian Electronics Industry Current Scenario Segment wise. Mobile Phone segment continually increasing growth it was Million Units sold of 96 in 2007-08 to 177.82 in 2011-12. CRT Television segment continually increasing growth it was Million Units sold of 15 in 2007-08 to 16.27 in 2011-12. LED

Television segment continually increasing growth it was Million Units sold of 2.27 in 2008-09 to 9.7 in 2011-12. MP3 Players segment continually increasing growth it was Million Units sold of 4.69 in 2007-08 to 8.5 in 2011-12. Set Top Boxes segment continually increasing growth it was Million Units sold of 3 in 2007-08 to 13.3 in 2011-12. Washing Machines segment continually increasing growth it was Million Units sold in 2.29 in 2007-08 to 5.27 in 2011-12. Passenger Cars segment continually increasing growth it was Million Units sold in 1.55 in 2007-08 to 3 in 2011-12. Two Wheelers segment continually increasing growth it was Million Units sold in 7.25 in 2007-08 to 14.83 in 2011-12.

9. The Electronic Component Industry:

While the demand for electronic equipment including Telecom, Consumer Durables, and IT sectors has witnessed sharp growth in India, the electronic component sector has lagged behind. The component industry depends on volumes for profitability and economies of large scale manufacturing. The Chinese have done extremely well on this count and high volume manufacturing of all types of electronic components has expanded there with new investments as well as re-location of factories from developed countries.

Electronic component manufacturing involves high value addition and thus is sensitive to finance, energy, infrastructure, logistics costs, all of which are high in India. This has resulted in the absence of a level playing field vis-à-vis our Asian competitors who have a very competitive eco-system for hi-tech manufacturing.

Various industry studies and estimates confirm that high value added (30-50% value addition) electronics manufacturing in India suffers 8-10% "disability costs" compared with competing countries. The higher the value addition, the higher the disability cost suffered by the manufacturer. This is also proved by the fact that new investments have been coming in low value added manufacturing activity rather than in components. The disabilities are as mentioned above- energy, finance, and infrastructure costs, plus the cascading taxes such as CST, or Local Government levies which are added to the cost of our components and products. Investments in capacity and technology have not been forthcoming and consequently, the economies of scale are missing.

The above scenario has resulted in a situation where imports of components have been growing rapidly and share of locally manufactured components used in equipment manufacturing has declined significantly since mid-90's and is currently about 39% of the total market. This does not include the derived demand for components which are being imported as part of finished electronic products. It is estimated that for a total electronics equipment market of USD 50 Billion, the total demand for components, used in manufacturing (or the Total Market) is expected to be between US$ 15-18 Billion.

10. Growth of Indian Electronic Components Industry:

The growth of the electronics industry has triggered the expansion of electronic component industry as well. The electronic components produced in India include, among others, Picture Tubes, Diodes, Transistors, Power devices, Resistors, Capacitors, Switches, Relays, Connectors, Magnetic heads, etc.

Table No. 7

Growth of Indian Electronic Components Industry

Year	Growth (in USD billions)
2007-08	7.6
2008-09	8.2
2009-10	9.2
2010-11	10.3
2011-12	11.8
2012-13	13.2
2013-14	14.8

Source: ELCINA, Dept. of Information Technology Ministry of Communications & Information Technology Govt. of India

Table no. 7 shows is Indian electronic components industry. The growth of the electronics industry continually increasing growth it was 7.6 in

2007-08 to 14.8 in 2013-14. The growth rate of 94.74% increase in Indian electronics components industry 2007-08 to 2012-13.

11. Indian Electronics Component Market:

The Indian electronic component market is dominated by electro-mechanical components (like printed circuit boards, connectors, etc.,) and passive components (like wound components, resistors, etc.). However, in recent times, the active components (like Integrated circuits, diode, etc.) and the associate components (like optical disc, magnets, RF Tuners etc.) have also witnessed significant growth.

Table No. 8

Indian Electronics Components Market

Type of Components	2007-08	2008-09	2009-10	2010-11	2011-12	2012-13	2013-14
Active Components	1.80	1.86 (4%)	24.20 (18%)	2.27 (3%)	2.51 (10%)	2.78 (11%)	3.09 (11%)
Passive Components	1.47	1.68 (14%)	1.88 (12%)	2.22 (18%)	2.63 (18%)	2.98 (15%)	3.36 (15%)
Electro-	2.16	2.30	2.46	2.84	3.27	3.63	4.03

Mechanical Components		(6%)	(7%)	(15%)	(15%)	(13%)	(13%)
Associate Components	2.09	2.35 (12%)	2.66 (13%)	3.02 (14%)	3.44 (14%)	3.82 (13%)	4.24 (13%)
Total	7.52	8.19 (7%)	9.20 (11%)	10.35 (11%)	11.85 (13%)	13.21 (12%)	14.72 (12%)

Source: ELCINA, Dept. of Information Technology Ministry of Communications & Information Technology Govt. of India

Table no. 8 shows in Indian electronics components market. Indian electronics components market compare to base year 2007-08. Active Components market increasing it was 4% in 2008-09, 18% in 2009-10, 3% 2010-11, 10% in 2011-12, and 11% in 2012-13 and 2013-14. Passive Components market increasing it was 14% in 2008-09, 12% in 2009-10, 18% in 2010-11 and 2011-12, and 15% in 2012-13 and 2013-14. Electro-Mechanical Components market increasing it was 6% in 2008-09, 7% in 2009-10, 15% in 2010-11 and 2011-12, and 13% in 2012-13 and 2013-14. Associate Components market increasing it was 12% in 2008-09, 13% in 2009-10, 14% in 2010-11 and 2011-12, and 13% in 2012-13 and 2013-14. All over components market highest increasing rate it was 13% in 2011-12 and lowest increasing rate it was 7% in 2008-09.

12. Overview of the Electronic Components Manufactured in India:

The below table no. 9 provides the details of the market size and growth along with import and local manufacturing information for most of the key components that comprise the electronic component market of India.

Table No. 9
Share of Electronics Components Manufactured in India   (USD Millions)

Components	Market Size		Imports		Production	
	2009-10	2010-2013 CAGR	2009-10	2010-2013 CAGR	2009-10	2010-2013 CAGR
Wound Components	1413	14%	989	6%	424	39%
Integrated Circuits	1163	12%	1097	13%	66	-
Cathode Ray Board (CRT)	789	12%	158	12%	631	1%2
Printed Circuit Board (PCB)	630	-1%	473	-4%	157	11%

Connector	607	8%	351	2%	256	19%
Speakers	409	7%	82	-19%	327	19%
Switch	377	12%	151	-4%	226	30%
Cables	373	12%	73	-22%	300	30%
Optical Disc	298	22%	60	22%	238	22%
Capacitor	269	11%	221	11%	48	11%
Magnets	110	-5%	99	-6%	11	5%
Diode	104	15%	84	15%	20	13%
Transistor	83	3%	66	3%	17	3%
Resistor	81	14%	59	20%	5	25%
LED	60	20%	55	20%	5	25%
Relays	31	9%	14	9%	17	9%
Fuse	15	7%	6	10%	9	6%
RF Tuners	100	10%	100	10%	Negligible Manufacturing	
Heat Sinks	67	7%	67	7%		
Piezo-electric crystal	63	13%	63	13%		
Magnetron	55	17%	55	17%		
Crystal Oscillator	54	8%	54	8%		
Micro/Stepper	22	9%	22	9%		

Motor						
Magnetic Tapes	10	5%	10	5%		
Other Components	2022	10%	1820	10%	202	5
Total Indian Electronic Component Market	9250	10%	-	-	-	-

Source: ELCINA, Dept. of Information Technology Ministry of Communications & Information Technology Govt. of India

13. Changing Trend in the Electronic Component Industry:

The electronic industry is going through an exciting phase with growth in demand and importance of electronics as well as revolutionary changes in technology, launch of innovative products and the challenge of global competition. This is coupled with the growing demand from all sectors of the economy for electronics driven by growing purchasing power. This has necessitated the electronic product and component manufacturers to focus on continuous improvement in their products in order to stay ahead of the pack. These have resulted in several interesting trends in the industry that make this sector exciting and meta-resources for all other sectors.

Convergence of Technologies:

Convergence of Technologies has become a reality in the last couple of years, the launch of main-line products enabling convergence. Convergence allows a single device to use multiple technologies/ services. A Smartphone is one of the key examples of the advent of convergence as it allows communication and computing using the same device. Convergence is moving beyond mobile phones to several other electronic devices like DVDs, music players, IPTV, I Pads etc. This trend is expected to convert most electronic products into multi-utility products, thereby, requiring high tech electronic components and technology.

Miniaturization:

The dawn of convergence has led manufacturers to integrate multiple devices. At the same time, the demand from consumers to reduce the size of the products to make them easy to manage has led to these products increasingly becoming smaller in size. Miniaturization refers to this creation of smaller scale devices or components for mechanical, optical, and electronic products &devices. Miniaturization results in greater density of components which is usually possible through VLSI designs. This also enables lower cost of production resulting in reduction in the overall product pricing.

Miniaturization is expected to increase and will impact the traditional component market as most of the traditional components shall be replaced by chip components and integrated Circuits.

Artificial Intelligence:

Consumers are becoming increasingly technology-conscious and are demanding products with built in intelligence. This is resulting in electronics and consumer durable products being manufactured with intelligent functions and logic. For example washing machines are now available that can sense the load and decide the appropriate washing cycles.

Intelligence has moved beyond consumer products and is also available in several medical electronics and industrial electronic products with CNC controlled functions. The above changes in the technology are expected to change the landscape for electronic component manufacturing. Apart from the above, manufacturers across the globe have started moving towards Green Electronics and sustainable development with implementation of RoHS (Restriction of Hazardous Substance) and WEEE (Waste electrical and electronic equipment's) regulations. In line with this trend, the Indian government too has issued notifications to regulate the use of Hazardous Substances (Lead, Cadmium, and Mercury etc.) and the proper disposal of WEEE. Similarly rules have also been notified with respect to energy efficiency norms and labeling of most consumer electronics and durables. The traditional components will increasingly face stiff competition from the Integrated Circuits and Surface Mount Technology (SMT) that will replace them in several electronic products. Therefore, in the near future, it is important for component manufacturers to shift focus from discrete components manufacturing to integrated components manufacturing so as to be able to benefit from the changing landscape of the country.

14. Electronics Production Scenario in India:

The Indian electronics industry has been broadly classified into two categories, namely IT Hardware & Electronics and Software. The production of IT (Hardware and Software) and electronics, which was worth about Rs 150 million in 1960, has increased to Rs 1730 million in 1971 and Rs 8900 million in 1981. It has further increased to Rs 94,344 million in 1991 and Rs 35, 01,300 million in 2008.

Table No. 10

Electronics Production Scenario in India:

Year	Production (Rs Crores)				Growth (%)		
	Total Electronic	Computer Software	Electronics Hardware	Electronics Hardware Production Share (%)	Total Electronic	Computer Software	Electronic Hardware
1991	9434	-	9434	-	-	-	-

1992	11016	-	11016	-	16.77	-	16.77
1993	14567	1550	13017	89.36	32.23	-	18.16
1994	17789	2351	15438	86.78	22.12	51.68	18.60
1995	21290	3900	17390	81.68	19.68	65.89	12.64
1996	25253	5700	19553	77.43	18.61	45.15	12.44
1997	30959	9300	21659	69.96	22.60	63.16	10.77
1998	39998	15200	24798	62.00	29.20	63.44	14.49
1999	50754	23000	27754	54.68	26.89	51.32	11.92
2000	68650	37550	31100	45.30	35.26	63.26	12.06
2001	76750	44600	32150	41.89	11.80	18.77	3.38
2002	92800	56000	36800	39.66	20.91	25.56	14.46
2003	113200	70500	42700	37.72	21.98	25.89	16.03
2004	145300	95500	49800	34.27	28.36	35.46	16.63
2005	178500	124000	54500	30.53	22.85	29.84	9.44
2006	231575	167175	64400	27.81	29.73	34.82	18.17
2007	282860	203060	79800	28.21	22.15	21.47	23.91
2008	350130	258000	92130	26.31	23.78	27.06	15.45

Source: Government of India Various Annual Reports, Department of Electronics, New Delhi

Table no. 10 show during the period 1991-2008, the electronics industry as a whole experienced an overall annual growth of 23.69 per cent. However, major growth can be traced to Indian software and services industry that grew at the annual rate of 40.63%, in comparison, the IT hardware and electronics sector experienced a moderate growth of only 14.34% during the same period. By 2008, the production of software and Services in India reached Rs. 25,80,000 crore. The Business Process Outsourcing (ITES-BPO) sector has emerged as a key driver of this phenomenal growth in the Indian software and services Sector.

It is of course, encouraging to note that in recent decade (2001-2008) IT hardware and electronics sector has experienced a higher growth than the last decade (1991-2000). But production of electronics and IT hardware as a proportion of total production in the electronics industry has been continuously declining as it declined from 45 percent in 2000 to 26 percent in 2008.

15. Sector wise Exports of Electronics Items:

The computer software industry has been one of the fastest growing sectors of the India. The uniqueness of the Indian software industry is that the industry possess hardware skills on the latest hardware platforms including IBM, main frame, As/400, DEC, HP, Unisys, DG, Unix Boxes, PC, MAC, PB/2, SUN and others.

Table No. 11

Sector wise Exports of Electronics Items

Item	2005-06	2006-07	2007-08	2008-09	2009-10	2010-11	2011-12
Consumer Electronics	2,000	1,500	1,600	2,600	3,000	1,400	1,227

Industrial Electronics	2,300	3,000	3,885	4,200	3,500	4,500	5,600
Computer Electronics	1,025	1,500	990	1,650	1,900	1,300	2,100
Communication & Broadcast Equipment	500	650	625	12,280	7,800	14,800	18,200
Electronics Components	3,800	5,850	6,100	10,500	9,700	18,400	15,500
Computer Software	1,04,100	1,41,000	1,64,400	2,16,190	2,37,000	2,68,610	3,32,769
Total	1,13,725	1,53,500	1,77,600	2,47,420	2,62,900	3,09,010	3,75,396

Source: Government of India Various Annual Reports, Department of Electronics, New Delhi

Table no. 11 shows the total exports of sector-wise electronics items continue increasing Rs. 113,725 crore in 2005-06, Rs.153,500 crore in 2006-07, Rs.177,600 crore in 2007-08, Rs.247,420 crore in 2008-09, Rs.262,900 crore in 2009-10, Rs. 309,010 crore in 2010-11, Rs. 375,396 crore in 2011-12. Consumer electronics increasing exports it was of Rs.2000 crore in 2005-06 and Rs. 3000 crore in 2009-10. And then after decreasing exports it was Rs. 1400 crore in 2010-11 and Rs. 1227 in 2011-12. Industrial electronics increasing exports it was of Rs. 2300 crore and Rs. 4200 crore. And then after exports it was Rs. 3500 in 2009-10 then increasing Rs. 4500 crore in 2010-11 and Rs. 5600 crore in 2011-12. A computer electronics export was fluctuating in year 2005-06 to 2011-12. Computer electronics increasing it was Rs. 1025 crore in 2005-06 and Rs.1500 crore in 2006-07 and then after decreasing it was Rs. 990 crore in 2007-08. Computer electronics exports it was Rs. 1650 crore in 2008-09, Rs. 1900 crore in 2009-10, Rs. 1300 crore in 2010-12 and Rs. 2100 crore in 2011-12. Communication & Broadcast equipment increasing exports it was Rs. 500 crore in 2005-06 and Rs. 12,280 crore in 2008-09 and then after decreasing exports it was Rs. 7,800 crore in 2009-10. Communication & Broadcast equipment increasing exports it was Rs. 14,800 crore in 2010-11 and Rs. 18,200 crore in 2011-12. Electronics components increasing exports it was Rs. 3,800 crore in 2005-06 and Rs. 18,400 crore in 2010-11 and then after decreasing it was Rs. 15,500 crore in 2011-12. Computer software increasing exports it was Rs. 104,100 crore in 2005-06 and Rs. 332,769 crore in 2011-12.

16. Classification of Electronics Industry Production Scenario:

1. Consumer Electronics Production:

The convergence of information, communication and entertainment is bringing new momentum in the consumer electronics industry in India. It has experienced rapid changes over the last few years. Changing life styles, higher disposable income and greater affordability is fuelling this growth. Consumer preference has shifted towards products and devices that come with smart technology, innovative designs and aesthetic looks. Premium products, particularly in the metros, are the growth drivers in the consumer electronics industry.

Table No. 12

Consumer Electronics Production

Year	Production (Rs. Crore)
2005-06	18,000
2006-07	20,000
2007-08	22,600
2008-09	25,550
2009-10	29,000
2010-11	32,000
2011-12	34,300
2012-13	41,200

Source: Department of Information Technology - Annual Report 2011-12 and Annual Report 2012-13

Chart No. 1

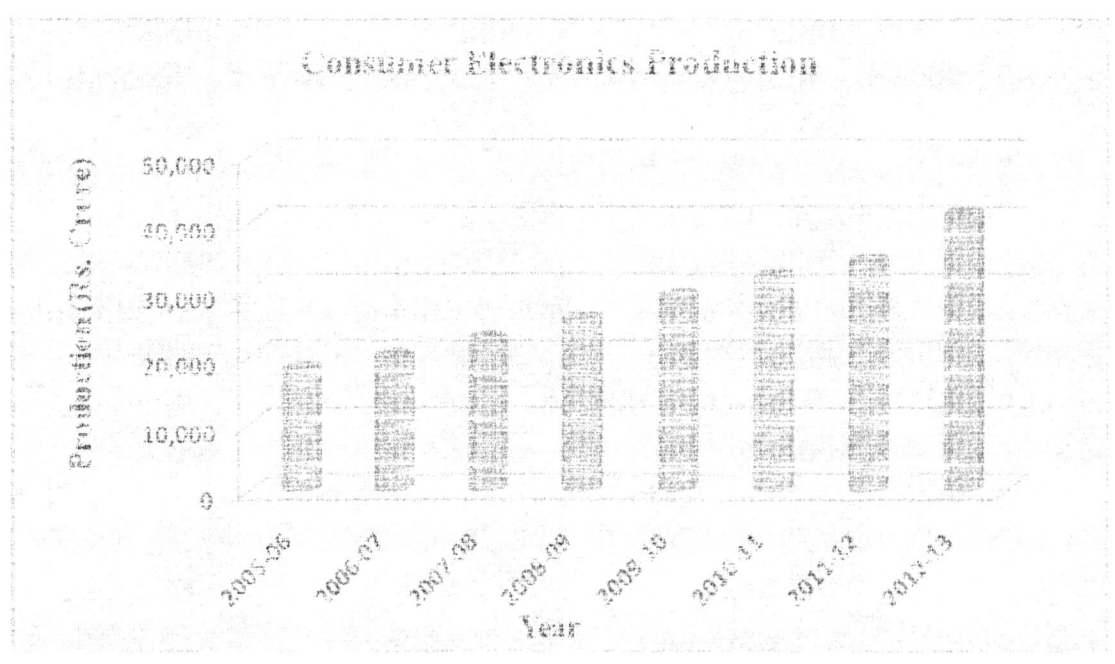

Table no.12 shows during 2010-11, the total production of consumer electronics is to be 32,000 Crore as against 29,000 Crore in 2009-10, a growth of about 10.34 per cent. During 2012-13 is estimated at 41,200 crore as against` 34,300 crore in 2011-12, growth of about 20%.

2. Industrial Electronics Production:

This segment of Electronics/IT industry includes critical hardware technologies and systems with built-in software. It is a very challenging area which is multi-disciplinary in nature requiring high level of technical skill in designing systems for applications in a variety of industrial sectors of the economy.

Whereas we have a good amount of expertise in conceptualizing such systems and its erection and commissioning, the sector is very largely dependent on import of critical hardware and associated software. Large projects are implemented with total import of C&I packages from abroad without any knowledge of its design. In most cases, this leads to higher initial cost and a much higher maintenance cost in the long run. This process is continuing for a long time now. The important devices used in this segment relate to power electronics, medical electronics and other intermediates like semiconductor. Semiconductors are integral part of most medical equipments, starting from high end imaging to small hand held devices.

Table No. 13

Industrial Electronics Production

Year	Production (Rs. Crore)
2005-06	8,800
2006-07	10,400
2007-08	11,910
2008-09	12,740
2009-10	15,160
2010-11	17,000
2011-12	18,700
2012-13	21,500

Source: Department of Information Technology - Annual Report 2011-12 and Annual Report 2012-13

Chart No. 2

Table no. 13 shows the production figure for this segment for 2010-11 is 17,000 Crore as against 15,160 Crore in 2009-10, a growth of about 12.14 per cent. During 2012-13 is estimated at 21,500 crore as against` 18,700 crore in 2011-12, growth of about 15%.

3. Computer Electronics Production:

India is one of the fastest-growing IT systems and hardware market in the Asia-Pacific region. Most of the prominent global vendors and some locals have strong presence in the Indian market. Most MNCs have their assembly units in India. BFSI (Banking, Financial Services and Insurance), telecom, ITeS (Information Technology enabled Services), manufacturing verticals, Small & Medium Enterprises (SMEs), e-Governance and households are the key drivers of the IT systems and hardware market in India. With significant IT adoption plans on the anvil, the IT systems and hardware market is expected to expand rapidly in the ensuing years.

PC sales are expected to record a growth of 12 per cent in 2010-11 to touch 9.7 million. The Notebook sales are estimated to be 3.5 million in 2010-11 against 2.5 million in 2009-10, a growth of 40 per cent. This shows that Notebooks have caught the fancy of the consumers. Desktop sales are expected to reach 6.2 million in 2010- 11 against 5.5 million in 2009-10, a growth of 12.7per cent. Notwithstanding this surge in PC sales, domestic production is estimated to remain flat in 2010-11 at 14,970 Crore. This is largely due to decelerating growth in exports, substitution of domestic production by cheaper imports and rising input cost.

Table No. 14

Computer Electronics Production

Year	Production (Rs. Crore)
2005-06	10,800
2006-07	12,800
2007-08	15,870
2008-09	13,490
2009-10	14,970
2010-11	14,970
2011-12	16,500
2012-13	24,300

Source: Department of Information Technology - Annual Report 2011-12 and Annual Report 2012-13

Chart No. 3

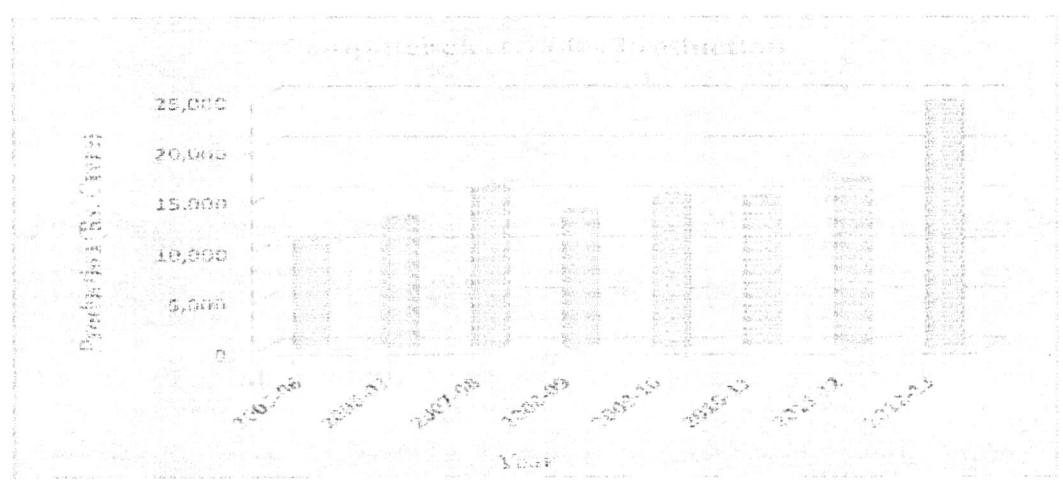

The derive value of production for this segment for 2012-13, is about 24,300 crore, as against 16,500 crore in 2011-12, a growth of about 47%.

4. Communication and Broadcasting Equipments Production:

Communication Technology is a key driver for development and growth. India is third largest in the world in terms of gross telephone subscribers, and second largest in Asia. The gross telephone subscribers in the country reached 787.28 Million at the end of December, 2010. Total wireless subscribers are 752.19 million as of December, 2010. The total Wire line subscribers are 35.09 million as of December, 2010. The overall Tele-density in India reached 66.16 per cent in December, 2010 with overall urban and rural Tele-densities being 147.88 and 31.18 respectively. The total broadband (256 kbps download) subscriber base of India is 10.92 million in December, 20

Table No. 15

Communication and Broadcasting Equipments Production

Year	Production (Rs. Crore)
2005-06	7,000
2006-07	9,500
2007-08	18,700
2008-09	26,600
2009-10	31,000

2010-11	35,400
2011-12	40,500
2012-13	55,000

Source: Department of Information Technology - Annual Report 2011-12 and Annual Report 2012-13

Chart No. 4

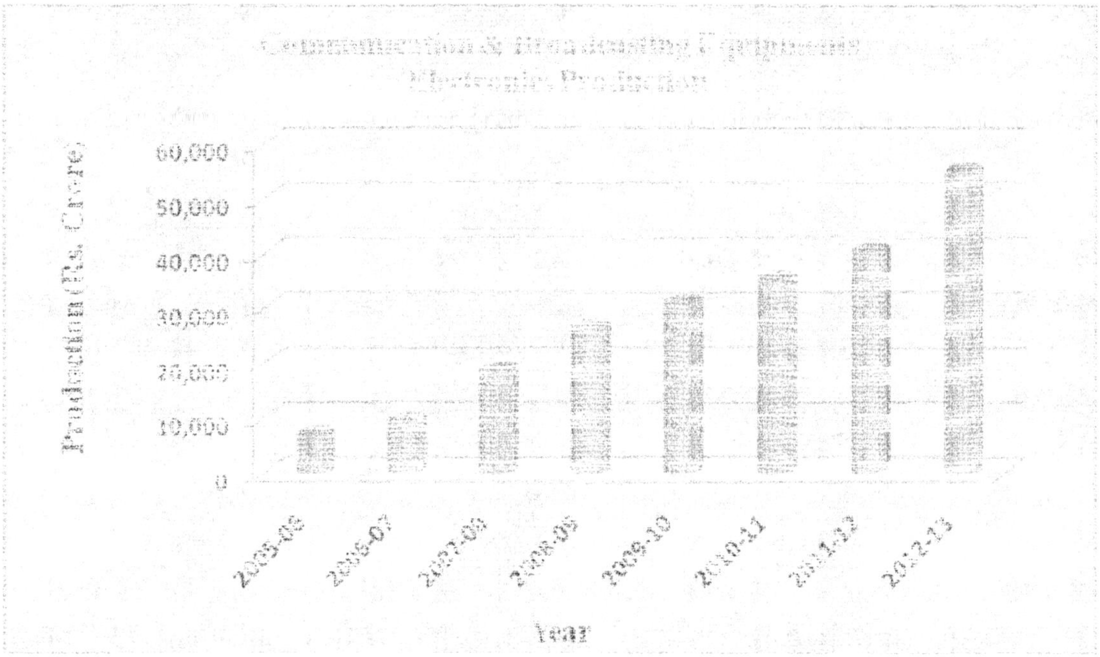

Table no. 15 shows the production figure for this segment for 2010-11 is 35,400 Crore as against 31,000 Crore in 2009-10, a growth of about 15 per cent. The estimated value of production for this segment for 2012-13 is 55,000 crore as against 40,500 crore in 2011-12, a growth of about 35.8%.

5. Strategic Electronics:

The strategic electronics segment envelops satellite based communication, navigation and surveillance system, radars, navigational aids, sonar's, underwater electronic system, infra-red based detection and ranging system, disaster management system, internal security system, etc. The Indian strategic electronic industry has been able to meet the bulk of the requirements of India's defense and paramilitary forces. India's defense, aerospace and nuclear sectors are poised for substantial growth on the back of economic growth and the need to maintain national and energy security. The role of IT in defense is expanding with the new focus on cyber security.

Driven by geo-political considerations, India is expected to be one of the top-5 markets for defense equipment by 2015. Similarly, economic growth and a focus by commercial aircraft manufacturers on low-cost countries are expected to create growth in the aerospace market in emerging markets in general and India in particular the civilian nuclear agreement. Between the US and India will enable commerce and cooperation, in particular allowing India to collaborate with global companies on nuclear projects. India has an opportunity to play an important role in this global phenomenon.

Table No. 16

Strategic Electronics Production

Year	Production (Rs. Crore)
2005-06	3,200
2006-07	4,500
2007-08	5,700
2008-09	6,840
2009-10	6,980
2010-11	7,700
2011-12	8,500
2012-13	9,000

Source: Department of Information Technology - Annual Report 2011-12 and Annual Report 2012-13

Chart No. 5

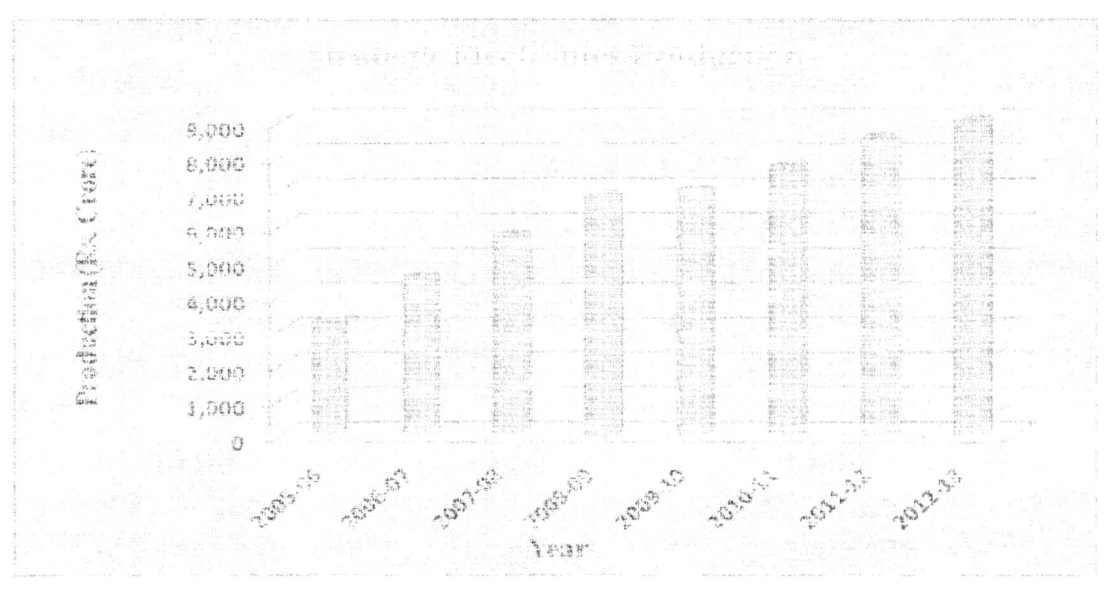

Table no. 16 shows the production figure for this segment for 2010-11 is 7,700 Crore as against 6,980 Crore in 2009-10, a growth of about 10 per cent. The derived value of production for this segment for 2012-13 is likely to be about 9,000 crore as against 8,500 crore in 2011-12, a growth of about 5.9%.

6. Electronic Components:

The total production of components was estimated at Rs. 88 billion during 2005-06. The colour picture tube production is likely to be around 11 million, a decline from 11.2 million in the last year. The production of B&W picture tubes declined further due to decreased market for B&W TVs. The components with major share in the export are CD-R, CPTs, PCBs, DVD-R, connectors, semiconductor devices, ferrites, resistors, etc. Significant developments took place during the year in the area of colour picture tubes and colour glass parts. Another CPT manufacturer successfully launched manufacture of pure flat tubes, leading to availability of flat tubes from three indigenous sources. The CPT units continued expansion of capacities to improve further their global competitiveness. Two more lines were commissioned during the year, one for manufacture of large size flat colour picture tubes and the second for small size. Two more lines are likely to come up next year. Keeping pace with the downward trend in prices of color TVs, the prices of CPTs also fell.

Table No. 17

Electronic Components

Year	Production (Rs. Crore)
2005-06	8,800
2006-07	8,800
2007-08	9,630
2008-09	12,040
2009-10	13,610
2010-11	21,800
2011-12	24,800
2012-13	26,500

Source: Department of Information Technology - Annual Report 2011-12 and Annual Report 2012-13

Chart No. 6

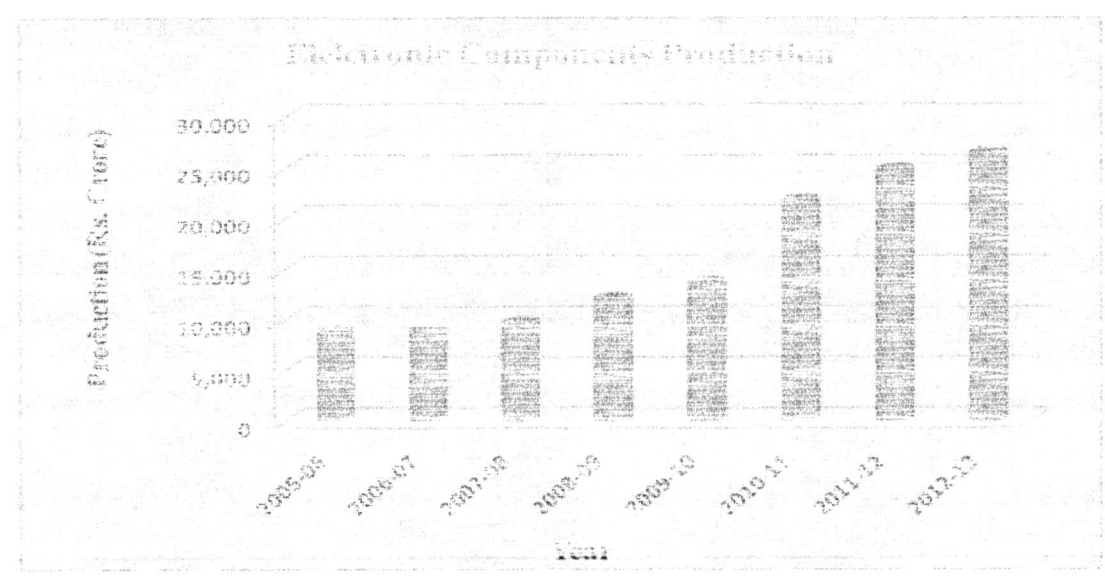

Table no. 17 shows the production figure for this segment for the year 2011-12 is to be around 24,800 crore as against 21,800 crore in 2010-11, registering a growth of about 14 per cent. The estimated production figure for this segment during is to the tune of 26,500 crore as against 24,800 crore in 2011-12, showing a growth of about 7 per cent.

CHAPTER 3
RESEARCH METHODOLOGY

1   INTRODUCTION

2   TITLE OF THE PROBLEM

3   SURVEY OF EXISTING LITERATURE

4   OBJECTIVE OF THE STUDY

5   HYPOTHESIS

6   SCOPE OF THE STUDY

7   UNIVERSE OF THE STUDY

8   SAMPLE DESIGNN

9   DATA COLLECTION

10 PERIOD OF THE STUDY

11 SIGNIFICANCE OF THE STUDY

12 STATISTIC TECHNIQUES

13 OUTLINE OF THE CHAPTER PLAN

14 LIMITATION OF THE STUDY

1. Introduction:

Research in common parlance refers to a search for knowledge. "As such the term 'research' refers to the systematic method consisting of enunciating the problems, formulating a hypothesis, collecting the facts or data, analyzing the facts and reaching certain conclusions either in the form of solutions towards the concerned problem or in certain generalizations for some theoretical formulation"[1]. In short, the search for knowledge through objective and systematic method of finding solution to a problem is research.

India has been one of the world's fastest growing economies during the last few years. The beginning of electronics was laid by physicists back in the 18th and 19th centuries. A big impetus was give by the electronics theory of conduction of metallic. It developed by many outstanding scientists in the late 19th and early 20th century. The electronics industry in India is about 35 years old. The period 1960-70 can be described as pre-liberalization period. The focus of policy during 1970 -80 was on developing indigenous Research & Development and capabilities. The next decade of 1970-80 witnessed a pronounced attempt at liberalization up to 1971; the electronics industry had grown up around three major centers Bangalore, Mumbai, Pune and Delhi. Presently it is focused on geographical spread.

Electronics characterizes as continuously changing technology global in nature production methods, market opportunities, distribution channels, service resources and competitive pressure. These highlight influence various sectors of economy as well as human life. According to Cherunilam Francis "Electronics is one of the most dynamic industry. Indeed the progress and efficiency of an economy depends to a large extent on application of electronics. The scope for application of electronics and advantages these from are enormous in a society. Electronics is indeed a pace setter"[2].

2. Title of the Problem:

My research topic is on the basis of Indian Electronics Industry. Now-a-days in India, Electronics characterizes as continuously changing technology global in nature of production methods, market opportunities, distribution channels, service resources and competitive pressure. These highlight influence various sectors of economy as well as human life. The main features of the Electronics industry is (1) Relatively pollution free (2) Knowledge incentive (3) Rapidly declining cost (4) Investment for balanced regional development in the country and (5) Global reach. I have to study all these aspect very deeply and clearly which is related to Profitability. My topic is on the basis of...

"Analysis of Profitability of Selected Electronics Industry in India"

3. Survey of Existing Literature:

John Myer, a renowned authority on Financial Statements Analysis, has referred that in the initial years of 20th century, the bankers and securities exchange authorities were extensively relying on the financial statements of the companies for analysis, monitoring and control of the activities and performance of businesses. The history, principles and financial statement analysis has been referred by another authority also: Kennedy and McMullen.

The most important pioneering books were written by **PODDAR** in 1962 and 1966 respectively, in which an attempt has been made to enumerate all the historical facts regarding various aspects of the industry. Some institutions like C.M.A. association of trade and industry, tariff commission, commerce research bureau, economics times, and national productivity council etc. Have made attempts to study the general problems in historical perspectives.

Dr. B. L. VARMA

He has written a book on analysis of financial statements. In this book he explain concept of financial statement easily and also provide all information about accounting techniques, statistical techniques and mathematical techniques. The case provides trend analysis, correlation, time series and analysis of variance. This is useful to this research area. In financial statement profitability, liquidity, ratio analysis is also indicating with the help of diagram.

SRINIVAS KOLLURU (2005)

The Indian steel industry has been showing tremendous improvements in terms of growth in capacity, production and exports and has become a major competitor in the global arena, thanks to the forces of deregulation and globalization. Keeping in view the current performance, the future looks bright for the domestic steel industry. India will be among the top 5 consumers of steel by 2010. The primary objective of this study is to measure an overall index of performance across the Indian steel companies based on eleven financial ratios including the profit ratio for each company by using the globally popular method – the Taxonomic Method. This method is preferred over the parametric methods using flexible functional forms and the Data Envelope Analysis (DEA). The empirical results show that, overall composite index would serve as a better performance indicator than the conventional stand-alone operating profit margin. Statistically speaking, the performance of eleven companies appeared to be converging during 1999-2003. The regression results reveal that the size factor - log (assets) - has been dominant. Contrary to conventional expectations the sign of market share shows positive and significant relation with overall performance. This is, perhaps, attributable to the price controls the steel industry has been subjected to for a long time before liberalization. Also, the larger companies are in the public sector excepting the TISCO. As a consequence, the expected U-shaped relationship between OPM/CPI turned to be counter-intuitively umbrella shaped.

DORON NISSIM & STEPHEN H. PENMAN (2001)

This paper presents a financial statement analysis that distinguishes leverage that arises in financing activities from leverage that arises in operations. The analysis yields two leveraging equations, one for borrowing to finance operations and one for borrowing in the course of operations. These leveraging equations describe how the two types of leverage affect book rates of return on equity. An empirical analysis shows that the financial statement analysis explains cross-sectional differences in current and future rates of return as well as in price-to-book ratios, which are based on expected rates of return on equity. The paper therefore concludes that balance sheet line items for operating liabilities are priced differently than those dealing with financing liabilities. Accordingly, financial statement analysis that distinguishes the two types of liabilities aids in the forecasting of future profitability and the evaluation of appropriate price-to-book ratios.

EHSAN H. FEROZ & RAYMOND L. RAAB (2003)

Ratio analysis is a commonly used analytical tool for verifying the performance of a firm. While ratios are easy to compute, which in part explains their wide appeal, their interpretation is problematic when two or more ratios provide conflicting signals. Indeed, ratio analysis is often criticized on the grounds of subjectivity that is the analysts must pick and choose ratios in order to assess the overall performance of a firm. In this paper, they demonstrate that Data Envelopment Analysis (DEA) can augment the traditional ratio analysis DEA can provide a consistent and reliable measure of the managerial or operational efficiency of the firm. They test the null hypothesis that there is no relationship between DEA and traditional accounting ratios as a measure of performance of a firm. Their results reject the null hypothesis indicating that DEA can provide information to analysts that is additional to that provided by the traditional ratio analysis. They illustrate the application of DEA to the oil and gas industry to demonstrate how financial analysts can employ DEA as a complement to ratio analysis.

KAURA AND SUBRAMANIAM (1979) published an article on the financial performance of 10 units relating to the period from 1972 to 1979 which mainly observed liquidity, profitability, financial structure and overall performance. For this study they used conventional ratio analysis and merit rating approach. They found that the financial strength of the units have declined over the years.

Dr. PRAMOD KUMAR (1991) published a book "Analysis of Financial statements of Indian industries" The study covered the 17 private, 5 state owned and 1 central public sector companies. He studied analysis of activities, assessment of profitability, return on capital investment, Analysis of financial structure, Analysis of fixed assets and working capital. In this book he revealed various problems of cement industries and suggested remedies for the problems. He also suggested for the improvement of profitability and techniques of cost control.

Mrs HEENA RAWAL (1999) studied the profitability of five District Milk Producers Co-Operative Union Ltd. of Gujarat State. She studied costing and pricing practice of milk co-operative of Gujarat State. They found that the profitability increase by reducing the cost or increasing the total sales. The co-operative has not adopted a proper costing system and Cost-Volume Profit method to control cost, Cost Centre has not been identified by any of the co-operative dairy.

Dr. S. J. PARMAR (2001) published a book in 2001. The book is a systematic study of the modern financial measurement techniques useful for management in planning and controlling corporate activities. With increasing participation by the general public and financial institutions as present and corporate bodies have to be on their guard and manage their efficient financial efficiency in the area of globalization. This book covers topics of concept and measurement of profitability, cost & sales trend, profit margin, assets turnover, analysis of return on investment common size of value added statements.

Dr. MISS KAILASH P. DAMOR (2002) has done research on "A comparative analysis of profitability trends in co-operative sugar industry of India" in the year 2002. In her research she has given clear idea about profit and profitability. Profit means; "it is an excess of Income over expenses." Profitability means "it is a capacity of earning profit." Profitability is related with two words, Profit and Ability. We discuss the word profit in many senses but the word profit is used as per its purpose, whereas the ability shows the capability of earning profit from business. Profitability also shows our capacity of how much return we can give to our investors on their investment.

Dr. SANJAY BHAYANI (2003) published a book in 2003 "Practical Financial Statement Analysis". The study covered 16 public limited Cement companies in private sector. He made study of analysis of Profitability, working capital, Capital structure and activity of Indian Cement industry. In his research he revealed various problems of Cement Industries and suggested remedied for the problem. He also suggested for the improvement of profitability and techniques of cost control.

Dr. RASIK N. BAVARIA (2004) has completed his research on "A comparative analysis of profitability vis-à-vis Liquidity performance in cement industry of India" in the year 2004. He has given importance of profitability and liquidity; by the term 'Liquidity' is meant the debt-repaying capacity of an undertaking. It refers to the firm's ability to meet the claims of suppliers of goods services and capital. Study of financial statement analysis is always made objectively. Generally, the external analyst uses the information as per his requirements. Financier would like to know profitability. Management would be interested in the operational efficiency and profitability. Position of the management profitability vis-à-vis liquidity should also balance in the portfolio. But if the management likes profitability, liquidity becomes less and if the liquidity is liked more the profitability gets less, for a short period of time. In the long run both will go together.

The most important book for electronics industry has written by **N. VITTAL** in 1996, with titled "**Indian incorporated reflections on the Indian Electronics Industry**" in which an attempt has been made to enumerate various views of industry.

Department of electronics, New Delhi published a book titled "**Guide to Electronics Industry in India**" in 1996. This describes outline of policy infrastructure, electronics manufacturers, production and export data with item name, quantity and value wise.

RAMCHANDRAN M. K. has studied on the aspect of working capital management in the electronics component industry in **KERALA** in 1996. Attempts have been made purely micro based study both side's electronics industry (component sector) and working capital management point of view.

RASTOGI RAJIV had written an article on **Indian Electronics Industry** in 1996 which describes the overall aspects of industry i.e.

policy, state public sectors state wise electronics production with share and classification criteria, state wise per-capita production, labor productivity and other related issues.

SHAH R. J. presented an article titled "**Status of Electronics Industry in Gujarat**" in 1997. This deals with various types of important information like production units and prospects of electronics industry in Gujarat.

RAMESH B. H., A case study of the Supreme Electronics Limited, Northern India. The Supreme electronics limited is engaged in the assembly of black and white, and color televisions sets, video cassette recorders, cassette, tapes, tape recorders, electronics calculators, transistor radios and two in one car stereos. Its factory is situates in a Cosmopolitan city in Northern India. The company was incorporated initially as private limited in late sixties and was converted into a public limited company in the year 1976 in pursuance of section 43A of the year 1980 its authorized capital and its paid up capital were Rs. 50 lacks and 23.15 lacks respectively. SEL is a closely held company and all the shares are held by the members of the same family.

SEL'S sales have shown an increasing trend during the period 1977-80. How're, the profitability of the company has been quite low. Accordingly it has become necessary the reasons for the decaling profitability of the company.

"A case study of Liquidity Management efficiency of Indian steel companies" by Dr. AMALENDY BHUNIA

The data used in the present study was acquired from CMIE database. All the private sector Indian steel companies were taken in this analysis. The sample is based on financial statements of the 230 Indian private sectors Steel companies of our economy, those who have often been neglected for enquiry and research. The used of a preferred sample of private sector might introduce a potential firm's success bias. It is claimed that the potential for success is overstated using this technique. The period covered by the study extends to 8years starting from 2002 to 2010. The reasons for restricting to this period were that the latest data for analysis was available for this period. Liquidity Management is crucial importance in financial management decision. The optimal of liquidity management is could be achieve by company that manage the tradeoff between profitability and liquidity management. The purpose of this study is to investigate the liquidity management efficiency and profitability relationship. A descriptive statistics discloses that liquidity and solvency position in terms of debt is very satisfactory and relatively efficient liquidity management is found but liquidity position has no impact on profitability.

CHAKRAVARTY AND REDDY had written an article on the financial performance of the industry for period from 1967 to 1971 by making comparison in 1973. They used ratio analysis as major tool for financial performance and had studied 22 ratios of profitability, proprietary, liquidity and turnover groups.

Dr. D. K. GHOSH studied the financial position of 18 private sector companies. Heaving paid up capital of Rs. 50 lacks or more. This study relates to the period from 1971-72 to 1975-76. His study is confined to the analysis of the balance-sheet, assets, and liabilities and condenses common size income and expenditure statement etc.

KAURA AND SUBRAMANIAM published an article on the financial performance of 10 units relating to the period from 1972 to 1979 which mainly observed liquidity, profitability, financial structure and overall performance. For this study they used conventional ratio analysis and merit rating approach. They found that the financial strength of the units have declined over the years.

BUTALAL C. AJMERA has done his dissertation **"Interpretation and analysis of Financial Statement of two selected units of Birla Group"** in the year 2001 by using conceptual framework of financial statement, research plan, profile of the cement industry. Birla group of companies a bird's eye view, liquidity position, financial structure and suggestion, the period of 1994-95 to1998-99. The study reveals the course of profitability.

"Liquidity, productivity and profitability of foreign banks and domestic banks in India, a comparative analysis", by **D. N. NAYAK**

described the high rate of growth in the business of foreign bank during the last decade. The performance of those banks in terms of other indicators like productivity and profitability made that group of banks a better performer than all other domestic banks in India.

ELJELLY, 2004 elucidated that efficient liquidity management involves planning and controlling current assets and current liabilities in such a manner that eliminates the risk of inability to meet due short-term obligations and avoids excessive investment in these assets. The relation between profitability and liquidity was examined, as measured by current ratio and cash gap (cash conversion cycle) on a sample of joint stock companies in Saudi Arabia using correlation and regression analysis. The study found that the cash conversion cycle was of more importance as a measure of liquidity than the current ratio that the affects profitability. The size variable was found to have significant effect on   profitability at the industry level. The results are liquidity management in various Saudi companies. First, it was clear that these was a negative relationship between profitability and liquidity indicators such as current ratio and cash gap in the Saudi sample examined. Second, the study also revealed that these were great variation among industries with respect to the significant measure of liquidity.

SMITH AND BEGEMANN 1997 emphasized that those who promoted working capital theory shored that **Profitability and Liquidity** comprised the salient goals of working capital management.

The problem arose because the maximization of the firms return could seriously threaten its liquidity and the pursuit of liquidity had a tendency to dilute returns. This article evaluated the association between traditional and return native working capital measures and return on investment (ROI), specifically industrial firms listed on the Johannesburg Stock Exchange (JSE). The problem under investigation was to establish whether the more recently developed alternative working capital concepts showed improved association with return on investment to that of traditional working capital ratios or not. Results indicated that there were no significant differences amongst the years with respect to the independent variables. The results of their stepwise regression corroborated that total current liabilities divided by funds flow accounted for most of the variability in returns on investment. The statistical test results showed that a traditional working capital leverage ratio, current liabilities divided by funds flows, displayed the greatest associations with return on investment. Well known liquidity concepts such as the current and quick ratios registered insignificant associations whilst only one of the newer working capital concepts, the comprehensive liquidity index, indicated significant associations with return on investment.

4. Objective of the Study:

The broad objectives of the study are to analyze the profitability of Electronics Industry in India. The objectives determine the future and outcome of the research. No one work is started without any objective. The objectives are as under:

1. To evaluate selected Electronics Companies annual accounts through appropriate ratios.

2. To examine profitability of Electronics Companies through different ratios.

3. To examine Financial Position of Electronics Companies in India.

4. To suggest ways and means to improve profitability without an addition of financial resources.

5. Hypothesis:

According to **Willion Emory**, "A hypothesis refers to propositions formulated for empirical testing." Ordinarily, when one talks about hypothesis, one simply means a mere assumption or some supposition to be proved or disproved. But for a researcher hypothesis is a formal question that he intends to resolve. Thus a hypothesis may be defined as a proposition or a set of propositions set forth as an explanation for the occurrence of some specified group of phenomena either asserted merely as a provisional conjecture to guide some investigation or accepted as highly probable in the light of established facts. Quite often a research hypothesis is predictive statement, capable of being tested by scientific methods, that relates an independent variable to some dependent variable.

"A hypothesis is a special proposition, formulated to be tested in a certain given situation as a part of research which states what the researcher is looking for?"[3]. In the research study, two hypotheses have been tested, these are as under:

Null hypothesis (Ho):

1. There is no significant difference in Operating Profit Ratio of selected Electronics Companies in India.

2. There is no significant difference in Gross Profit Ratio of selected Electronics Companies in India.

3. There is no significant difference in Return on Capital Employed of selected Electronics Companies in India.

4. There is no significant difference in Net Profit Ratio of selected Electronics Companies in India.

5. There is no significant difference in Return on Net Worth of selected Electronics Companies in India.

6. There is no significant difference in Earning Per Share of selected Electronics Companies in India.

7. There is no significant difference in Dividend Payout Ratio of selected Electronics Companies in India.

Alternative Hypothesis (H₁):

1. There is significant difference in Operating Profit Ratio of selected Electronics Companies in India.

2. There is significant difference in Gross Profit Ratio of selected Electronics Companies in India.

3. There is significant difference in Return on Capital Employed of selected Electronics Companies in India.

4. There is significant difference in Net Profit Ratio of selected Electronics Companies in India.

5. There is significant difference in Return on Net Worth of selected Electronics Companies in India.

6. There is significant difference in Earning Per Share of selected Electronics Companies in India.

7. There is significant difference in Dividend Payout Ratio of selected Electronics Companies in India.

6. Scope of the Study:

The scope of this research study is as under.

Functional Scope

Functional scope of this study is to analyze Profitability of Indian Electronics industry.

Geographical Scope

In this study researcher selected 5 Electronics Industry which are working and producing in India. So, whole India is geographical criteria for this research study.

7. Universe of the Study:

The universe of the study consists of the electronics industry working in India and listed in stock exchanges of India.

8. Sampling Design:

There are many electronics industry which are working in India. In this research study, researcher has randomly selected 5 Electronics Industry as the sample for this study. The sample has been selected considering following factors:

- The companies are established in before 10 years.
- Data for the entire period of the study from 2003-04 to 2012-13 are available.
- The companies should be listed in Indian Stock Exchange.

List of Electronics Industry is listed in Indian Stock Exchange:

- Bharat Electronics Ltd.
- Delta Electronics Ltd.
- Digital Electronics Ltd.
- Blue Star Ltd.
- BPL Ltd.
- Electronics Corporation India Ltd.
- Gujarat –Poly-Avt Electronics Ltd.
- JCT Electronics Ltd.
- Centum Electronics Ltd.

- Panasonic Home Appliance India Co. Ltd.

- Philips Electronics India Ltd.

- Deltron Ltd.

- Precision Electronics Ltd.

- Procal Electronics India Ltd.

- Solzer Electronics Ltd

- MIRC Electronics Ltd.

- Pan Electronics India Ltd.

- Starvox Electronics Ltd.

- Trend Electronics Ltd.

- TVS Electronics Ltd.

- Videocon Industries Ltd.

- Zicom Electronics Securities Systems Ltd.

List of selected 5 Electronics Industry which are given below:

1. Bharat Electronics Ltd.

2. Centum Electronics Ltd.

3. MIRC Electronics Ltd.

4. TVS Electronics Ltd.

5. Blue Star Ltd.

9. Data Collection:

The data collection is very important task for the researcher for the research study. This research study is mainly based on secondary data. The secondary data shall be collected from the records, documents, related subject matter and related web side. Personal visits and unstructured interviews with the officials of the electronics constitute are also the main source of the data. Besides, the researcher shall collect and analyze published data as per the requirement.

As such the universe of this research study is restricted with the reference to selected Electronics Industry, which is working in India. So, researcher has selected 5 Electronics Industry. The data regarding selected 5 Electronics Industry have been obtained and collected from the annual report of the Electronics Industry and related websites.

10. Period of the Study:

This research study covered the data of last ten years of the functioning of the selected electronics units. A longer period could have been still better but due to time and resource constraints the last ten years not very short period has been taken for analyze the data of research program. The study period is ten years, starting from year 2003-04 to 2012-13.

11. Significance of the Study:

Significance of the study is as under:

Contribution to the knowledge:

➤ Through this research study the knowledge of researcher particularly regarding statistical tools and technique and statistical test improve.

➢ The knowledge regarding electronics industry will be improved.

Contribution to the society:

➢ Through this research study society will be able to know the real situation of profitability of the electronics industry in India.

➢ Society will be able to know the appropriate various profitability ratios.

Contribution to the Industry:

➢ Electronics Industry may be able to know the profitability with the help of data interpretation.

➢ Electronics Industry will try to improve their financial performance.

12. Accounting and Statistical Techniques:

The main base of the study is to analyze profitability of the selected Electronics Industry. Verifying and testing this hypothesis, some techniques have been used. Here, mainly applied test or techniques are as under.

12.1 Accounting Technique:

Accounting techniques or tool which may use for financial analysis is such as ratio analysis. The users pick up the techniques to suit their requirements and also on the basis of data available to them.

Ratio Analysis:

Ratio is useful analysis for financial statement. It is conveniently and clearly capsules the data in a form that is easily understood interpreted as "Ratios are simply a means of highlighting in arithmetical terms, the relationship between figures drawn from financial statements". The technique of ratio analysis is the process of determining and interpreting numerical relationship based on the financial statements.

According to Batty "Accounting ratio describes the significant relationship which exists between figures shown in a Balance sheet, in a Profit & Loss account, in a budgetary control system, another part of accounting or organizing".

It concludes whether the financial condition of a business enterprise is good or bad it is universally used for appraising the performance of a business firm.

12.2 Statistical Techniques:

Use of statistical techniques has become a normal phenomenon in any type of analysis.

Average / Mean:

"The most commonly used average is the arithmetic mean, briefly referred to as the mean." The mean can be found by adding all the variables and dividing it by total number of the years taken. It gives a brief picture of a large group which is represents and gives a basic of comparison with other groups. The formula of mean is as under.

$$\overline{X} = \frac{\Sigma X}{n}$$

The Standard Deviation:

The Standard deviation concept was introduced by **Karl Pearson** in 1823. It is by far the most important and widely used measure of studying dispersion. Standard deviation is also known as root mean square deviation for the reason that it is the square root of the mean of the square deviation from arithmetic mean. The formula of standard deviation is as under.

$$\sigma = \sqrt{\frac{\Sigma \left(X - \overline{x} \right)^2}{n-1}}$$

Diagrammatic and Graphic presentation of data:

Diagrams and Graphs are visual aids, which give a bird's eye of a given set of numerical data. They present the data in comprehensible and intelligible from. Graphic presentation of statistical data gives a pictorial effect to what would otherwise be just a mass of figures. Diagrams and graphs depict more information than the data presented in the tabular from. These clarify the existing trend in the data and how the trend changes.

For presenting the data of sampled banks, diagrammatic and graphic presentation of data have been applied.

ANOVA (Analysis of Variances):

What is ANNOVA?

Professor **R. A. Fisher** was the first man to use the term 'Variance' and in fact, it was he who developed a very elaborate theory concerning ANNOVA, explaining its usefulness in practical field. Later on Professor Snedecor and many others contributed to the development of this technique. ANNOVA is essentially a procedure for testing the different group of data for homogeneity. "The essence of ANNOVA is that the total amount of variation in a set of data is broken down into two types, that amount which can be attributed to chance and that amount which can be attributed to specified causes". There may be variation between sample and also within sample items. ANNOVA consists in splitting the variance for analytical purposes. Hence, it is a method of analysis the variance to which a response is subject into its various components corresponding to various sources of variation.

One - way ANNOVA

Under the one-way ANOVA, we consider only one factor and that the reason for said factor to be important is that several possible types of samples can occur within that factor. We then determine if there are differences within that factor. The technique involves the following table.

F-test is also known as ANOVA, means analysis of variances.

Table No. 3.1

Analysis of Variance Table for One-way ANOVA

Source of Variation	Sum of Squares (SS)	Degree of Freedom (d.f)	Mean Square (MS)	F-ratio
Between Samples	$\Sigma \dfrac{(Tj)2}{nj} - \dfrac{(T)2}{n}$	$(k - 1)$	$\dfrac{SS\ between}{(k-1)}$	$\dfrac{MS\ between}{MS\ within}$
Within Samples	$\sum X^2_{ij} - \Sigma \dfrac{(Tj)2}{nj}$	$(n - k)$	$\dfrac{SS\ within}{(n-k)}$	
Total	$\sum X^2_{ij} - \dfrac{(T)^2}{n}$	$(n - 1)$		

Source: "Research Methodology" by Kothari C. R., second edition, p. 311

n = total number of items in all the samples

k = number of samples

13 Outline of Chapter Plan:

The present study is divided into six chapters, which are as under:

Chapter - 1 Conceptual Framework of Profitability

In this chapter analysis of profitability of Electronics units under study has been explained. Here concept of profit and profitability, factors affecting the profitability, Significance of profitability, techniques to measure profitability, concept of ratio analysis, purpose and types of ratios, importance of ratio analysis, benefits of ratio analysis, limitations of ratio analysis has been discussed.

Chapter: 2   Overview of Electronics Industry

A brief history of electronics industry, which includes the introduction, classification of electronics industry, global electronics production scenario, growth rates of the global electronics industry by region, goods importers & exporters in the electronics industry, global value chains in the electronics industry, electronics industry in India, Indian electronics industry-current scenario, the electronics component industry, growth of Indian electronics components industry, India electronics component market, overview of the electronics components manufactured in India, changing trend in the electronics component industry, electronics production scenario in India, sector wise exports of electronics items, classification of electronics industry production scenario.

Chapter: 3   Research Methodology

In this chapter includes, Introduction, Title of the Research Problem, Survey of the Literature, Objectives of the study, Hypothesis, Sampling Design, Scope of the study, Sampling Design, Universe of the study, Data collection, Period of the study, Tools and Techniques for analysis of Profitability, Outline of the Chapter Plan, & Limitations of the study.

Chapter: 4 Sample Profile

The fourth chapter of my research work is sample profile. In this chapter researcher has talked about all selected Electronics Companies. Its history, growth and present situation so on.

Chapter: 5 Analysis of Profitability

In this chapter analysis of profitability of Electronics units under study has been explained. A study of Profitability of Selected Electronics units to use various statistical tools and techniques ratio analysis and also include F-test (ANOVA) Analysis and deep study has been done and at last result should be received.

Chapter: 6 Summary, Findings and Suggestions

This chapter gives its emerging conclusion based on the analysis carried out and points out the variation any from the literature. It also gives concrete suggestions for enhancing Financial Performance, profitability for financial soundless and cost control.

15 Limitation of the Study:
The limitations of the present study are as under.

1. Scope of this study is wider but sample size is limited to only 5 Electronics units are covered in this study only.

2. This research study based on secondary data collected from annual reports of various 5 Electronics units and related websites. The

limitation of the secondary data and its findings depend entirely on the accuracy of such data.

3. The data, which is used for his study is based on annual report of the 5 Electronics units and secondary data collected from published reports from time to time. Therefore the quality of this research depends on quality and reliability of data published in annual reports.

4. There are deferent approaches to measure the profitability in this regard expert views differ from one other.

5. The different views have been applied in the calculation of different ratios.

6. The present study is largely based on ratio analysis. It has its own limitations.

CHAPTER 4
SAMPLE PROFILE

1. ELECTRONICS COMPANIES PROFILE:

1. Bharat Electronics Limited

2. Centum Electronics Limited

3. MIRC Electronics Limited

4. TVS Electronics Limited

5. Blue Star Limited

1. ELECTRONICS COMPANIES PROFILE:

Electronics is distinct from electrical and electro-mechanical science and technology, which deals with the generation, distribution, switching, storage, and conversion of electrical energy to and from other energy forms using wires, motors, generators, batteries, switches, relays, transformers, resistors, and other passive components. This distinction started around 1906 with the invention by **Lee De Forest** of the triode, which made electrical amplification of weak radio signals and audio signals possible with a non-mechanical device. Until 1950 this field was called "Radio Technology" because its principal application was the design and theory of radio transmitters, receivers, and vacuum tubes.

A big impetus was given by the electronics theory of conduction of metallic. In the primary era of electronics (1887-1900) business concern with mainly Radio Communication and Telegraph companies. It developed by many outstanding scientists in the late 19th and early 20th century. In early 1920['s] electronics accounts for an important percentage of national GDP with represents a growing proportion of world's production.

The Indian electronics industry has been in the forefront of the Indian manufacturing revolution. Recently the industry has witnessed higher growth due to consistent and high rate of market growth as well as several government policy changes to encourage manufacturing by ironing out the anomalies in the tax system. The electronic industry is going through an exciting phase with growth in demand and importance of electronics as well as revolutionary changes in technology, launch of innovative products and the challenge of global competition. This is coupled with the growing demand from all sectors of the economy for electronics driven by growing purchasing power. This has necessitated the electronic product and component manufacturers to focus on continuous improvement in their products in order to stay ahead of the pack. These have resulted in several interesting trends in the industry that make this sector exciting and meta-resources for all other sectors.

2. PROFILE OF THE ELECTRONICS COMPANIES:

1. Bharat Electronics Limited

Type	: State-owned
Enterprise	: Public company
Traded as BSE	: 500049
NSE	: BEL
Founded	: Bangalore, India (1954)
Headquarters	: Bangalore, India
Number of Locations	: 9 factories

Key People   : Shri S. K. Sharma (Chairman and MD)

Revenue   : 10 Rupees (2012)

Net Income   : 1252.46 Crore (2012-13)

Total Equity   : 80 Crore (2012-13)

Total Assets   : 6322.86 Crore (2012-13)

Employees   : 11,961 (March 2009)

Website   : www.bel-india.com

History:

Bharat Electronics Limited (BEL) was incorporated in 1954; it is engaged in manufacturing of defence electronics and other electronic equipments. In 1956 BEL manufactured communication equipment. Later it produced receiving valves in 1961, germanium semiconductors in 1962 and radio transmitters for AIR in 1964.

During 1960s and 1970s it manufactured Transmitting Tubes, Silicon Devices Integrated Circuits, Black and White TV Picture Tube, X-ray Tube, Microwave Tubes, TV Transmitters for Doordarshan and Frigate Radars for the Navy. Between 1980s and 1990s it manufactured equipments such as large scale low power TV transmitters and TVROs for the expansion of Doordarshan's coverage, Electronic Warfare Equipment and many more.

Today it has a wide range of product portfolio that caters to defence, non defence and it also provides systems and turnkey solutions.

It has manufacturing facilities located Panchkula, Ghaziabad, Kotdwara, Navi Mumbai, Pune, Hyderabad, Machilpatnam, Chennai and Bangalore.

Products:

Defence- It manufactures products like communications, radars, naval system, opto electronics, electronic warfare systems, tank electronics and simulators.

Non Defence- Switching equipments, DTH, simputer, electronic voting machine, electronic components.

Under System and Turnkey solution it provides solutions for map survey, radio path survey, configuration, access systems, antenna etc.

It also offers services such as contract manufacturing, software development, semiconductor device packaging etc.

Recent Development:

Bharat Electronics is forming some joint ventures to achieve technical excellence. Bharat Electronics Limited has set up a Joint Venture with General Electric (GE) USA, for manufacturing high voltage tanks and detector modules for Computed Tomography (CT) scan systems and advanced level of X-ray tubes. The company is in the process of joining with BHEL (Bharat Heavy Electricals Limited) to set up a joint venture to make solar photovoltaic components. BEL has signed a memorandum of understanding (MOU) with Indus Teqsite, Chennai for the design and development of digital subsystems for its equipment, test systems for its radars, avionics and electronic warfare. BEL signed another MOU with a French company Thales International to set up a joint venture for civilian and defense Radars. BEL has signed and MOU with Textron Systems, for providing Micro-observer Unattended Ground Sensor (UGS) systems to the Indian security agencies.

Financial Indicators:

As per the report published by Crisil research on 21 April 2011 the revenue of company has increased but EBITDA margins have reduced significantly from 24.6% in March 2009 to 16.8% in March 2010. In revenue it is quite bigger than its peer competitors like Astra Microware Products Limited, Gemini Communications Limited and Sterlite Technologies Limited. BEL's EBITDA margin is lower than Astra and Gemini though they are small in size. The reason for increased top line growth is the increased expenditure on defense by Government of India. Last three years PAT remains stable because of lower interest rate and forex gain of close to Rs 700 million compared to forex loss in FY 09 of Rs 445.2 million.

2. Centum Electronics Limited

Founded   : 1994

Trade as BSE   : 517544

Trade as NSE	: CENTUM
Founded by	: Mr. Apparao Mallavarapu
Headquarter	: Bangalore
Products	: Consumer, Medical, Strategic Electronics, Communications, Automotive and Industrial Segments.
Locations	: 4 in Bangalor
Net Income	: 2.85 Crore (2012-13)
Total Equity	: 12.37 Crore (2012-13)
Total Assets	: 110.28 Crore (2012-13)
Chairman & Managing Director	: Krishnan, P Rama Rao, Manoj Nagrath, Rajiv C Mody
Company Secretary	: Ramu Akkili
Website	: www. centumindia.com

History: Centum Electronics was founded in 1994 by Mr. Apparao Mallavarapu in Bangalore, India. Since then, Centum has rapidly grown into a diversified electronics company operating across different industry segments and offering a broad range of products and services. It has continuously invested in strengthening its design & product development capabilities and has established truly world-class manufacturing facilities which today are spread across 4 locations in Bangalore.

A key contributor to Centum's growth has been the strong relationships forged with international customers and partners that have enabled the company to establish a global presence and bring value to a range of customers. This customer-focused approach coupled with Centum's core-values of Technology-Teamwork-Trust has resulted in a track-record of high quality products & services and excellent execution ability.

Company Background:

Centum Electronics Limited (Centum) designs, manufactures and also exports electronic products. These include subsystems, modules, box builds, besides complex electronic components. Centum serves customers engaged in mission critical solutions with advanced tailor-made technologies. These range from Strategic Electronics (Space, Defense and Aerospace) to Industrial, Communications, and Medical.

Centum has been steadily increasing its product and service range, geographical reach and catering to increased industry segments in its goal to expand its offerings and become the sophisticated one stop shop OEMs are seeking. With extensive design & development expertise and leading-edge enabling technologies Centum is now the industry leader in India in electronics solutions &components.

The strategy over the years has been consistent and is based on high customer focus with competent people, state of the art technology and high quality products. Centum's vision is "To Create Value by contributing to the Success of its Customers, by providing best-in-class Electronics Design and Manufacturing Solutions in high technology areas."

Industry Structure and Development:

Broadly, the electronics industry is categorized under Consumer, Medical, Strategic Electronics, Communications, Automotive and Industrial segments.

Government of India has recognized the importance of Electronic industry and announced the National Electronics Policy (NEP). The demand of the Indian market is expected to reach USD 400 Billion by 2020. At the current growth rate, the domestic production is expected to reach USD 100 Billion leaving a gap of USD 300 Billion. The Government's vision is to create a globally competitive Electronics System Design and Manufacturing (ESDM) industry to meet the country's needs and serve the international markets. To meet this vision, the Government has introduced a scheme for Electronics Manufacturing Cluster (EMC) to ensure world class infrastructure and facilities to be provided to attract investments. Accordingly, the Government has decided to offer financial support in the formation of EMCs. Further to attract investments, the Government has introduced Modified Special

Incentive Package Scheme (MSIPS)http://deity.gov.in for new and expansion of existing units. This scheme offers an incentive up to 25% of the value of investment in Plant and Machinery. We hope the focus given by the Government of India will create many more opportunities in the ESDM sector.

As a company we operate in Strategic Electronics, Communication, Industrial and Medical industry segments.

3. MIRC Electronics Limited

Industry Type   : Consumer electronics

Founded   : 1981

Trade as BSE   : 500279

Trade as NSE   : MIRCELECTR

Headquarters   : Mumbai, Maharashtra, India

Revenue   : 15284.6 million (US$260 million)

Net Income   : 7.63 Crore (2012-13)

Total Equity   : 14.19 Crore (2012-13)

Total Assets   : 311.77 Crore (2012-13)

Employees   : 1500

Website   : www.onida.com

History : MIRC Electronics incorporated in 1981 is engaged in manufacturing and marketing of LCD TV, DVD and home theatres, air conditioner, washing machine, mobile phone, microwave oven and projectors and display products. The company was founded by Mr. G. L. Mirchandani and Mr. Vijay Mansukhani. Company markets its products under the brand name 'ONIDA'. It is part of the Onida group, which also includes which includes the associate companies Monica Electronics, Onida Credit & Investment, Onida Finance, Vaka Electronics, OFL Capital Corporation, Onida Saka, Onida International, and OFL Securities. Company's manufacturing plant is located at Thane, Noida and Roorkee. Today the company has network of 33 branch offices, 208 Customer Relation Center's and 41 depots spread across the country. Company produces single color television in 12 seconds and has manufacturing capacity of 1.2 million sets in a year. The company has set up installed capacities of 3 million television sets, 100,000 air conditioners, 380,000 washing machines, and 3.72 million electronic tuners. A team of dedicated engineers works at the Onida research and development centers in Mumbai and Delhi conducting research in the areas of embedded software, industrial design, mechanical engineering, electrical engineering, and model shop. The company also has sales and marketing office in Dubai. Mirc Electronics exports its products to Uganda, Tanzania, Kenya and Ethiopia and SAARC countries. Company is marketed in big hypermarkets like Lu

Centers, Carrefour's, Geants and Desmans in GCC countries. MIRC Electronics shares are listed on the National Stock Exchanges and Bombay Stock Exchanges.

Products:

- LCD TV
- Television
- DVD and Home Theatres
- Air Conditioning
- Washing Machine
- Mobile Phones
- Microwave Oven
- Projectors and Display Product

Future Plans:

MIRC Electronics expects to increase its presence in their product portfolio and emerge as a leading solutions provider for electronic home improvement good. The Company has also introduced a high tech world class LCD which is considered the best in the industry.

4. TVS Electronics Limited

Type   : Public Limited

Industry   : Electronics and Manufacturing

Founded   : 1986

Trade as BSE : 532513

Trade as NSE	: TVSELECT
Headquarters	: Chennai, India
Key People	: Gopal Srinivasan, Director
Products	: Computer peripherals, Printers, Key boards, UPS IT Services
Net Income	: 10.8 Crore (2012-13)
Total Equity	: 17.67 Crore (2012-13)
Total Assets	: 99.70 Crore (2012-13)
Website	: www.tvs-e.in

History :TVS Electronics Ltd is one of the premier IT Peripherals companies in India. The company is a part of the 99-year-old, USD 3.5 billion TVS Group, one of India's oldest & most trusted business groups. They are engaged in the business of transaction automation information technology (IT) products and solutions. The company has two subsidiary companies, namely Tumkur Property Holdings Ltd and Prime Property Holdings Ltd. The company is a subsidiary of TVS Investments Ltd. Sundaram-Clayton Ltd is the ultimate holding company. The company is headquartered in Chennai. The company is having their manufacturing unit located at in Dehradun, Uttarakhand. They are having the partner network comprising of 3500+ authorized dealer partners and 400+ authorized service partners covering

450+ towns. The company's principal products include computer peripherals and IT management services. Their other products include receipt printers, which includes RP-45 Shoppe, RP-35, RP-3160 and RP-3200; automatic identification and data capture/collection (AIDC) products, which includes LP-44, LP-46, BS-C101 Star, BS-L1010 Platina, and point of sale (POS) accessories, which includes PD-VFD, MSR-104, POS-60, Cash Drawer and Paper Roll. TVS Electronics Ltd was incorporated on September 15, 1995. The company was formerly known as TVS e-Technology Ltd. Initially, the company was a national player in the customer support, technology support and maintenance services (TMS) areas. They offered field customer support to products of TVS-E. Also, they acted as a preferred outsourced strategic partner for various Brand Owners / Service Providers.

Products of the Company:

- POS Systems & Terminals
- Receipt Printers
- Invoice Printers
- Barcode Label Printers
- Barcode Scanners
- POS Accessories
- Keyboards
- Report Printers
- Institutional Products

- Supplies

Awards & Recognitions:

- North East Compu VAR Awards for 3rd year in a row for the Best DMP brand

- TVS–E accredited with ISO 9001:2008 certificate

- TVS–E accredited with ISO 14001:2004 certificate

- MAIT Recognition for Business Excellence, (Level II)– 2003 and MAIT recognition for excellence in Exports during the year 2002–03

- A ranking in First 250 of Deloitte Touche Tohmatsu's Asia–Pacific Technology Fast 500.PC

- Quest User's choice Award 2001 & 2000–awarded to Dot Matrix Printers

- MAIT Recognition for excellence in exports for the year 2001 – 02, 1999–2000, 1998–99. MAIT Quality Recognition

- Programmer Level 1 for UPS (1998 & 99) & for Printers division (1997). Elcina award for

- Excellence in Quality 1999–2000 and Excellence in R&D 97–98.Preferred Vendor Crompton

- Greaves Award 1998–1999 by Telecom division (PSTA Unit) Jigani, Bangalore

- Information system award (Techies '97) by Computer World. Best Seller: Dot Matrix Printers.

- Victron BV Supplier 1997: Preferred Supplier Award

- Elcina electronics Man of the Year award 1996–97 to Gopal Srinivasan, Director TVS–E

5. Blue Star Limited

Founded	: Mumbai, India (1943)
Trade as BSE	: 500067
Trade as NSE	: BLUESTARCO
Enterprise	: Public Limited
Headquarters	: Mumbai, India
Manufacturing Units	: 7
Offices	: 30
Dealers	: 1800+
Net Income	: 135.35 Crore (2012-13)
Total Equity	: 17.99 Crore (2012-13)
Total Assets	: 867.05 Crore (2012-13)
Employees	: 2700
Website	: bluestarindia.co
History	:

Blue Star Limited (originally known as Blue Star Engineering (Bombay) Pvt. Ltd) was founded by Mohan T Advani in 1943. The Company was initially engaged in reconditioning of refrigerators and air-conditioners.

Today, Blue Star is India's largest central air-conditioning company with an annual turnover of Rs 1607 Crores, a network of offices in 30 cities in India, and four modern manufacturing facilities. Blue Star became a public limited company in 1969 with its corporate headquarters at Kasturi Building in Mumbai.

Blue Star manufactures and markets a wide range of air-conditioning and refrigeration systems and products. These include large central air-conditioning plants, packaged air-conditioning systems, split and window air-conditioners; commercial refrigeration equipment such as water coolers, bottled water dispensers, ice-cube machines, deep freezers and walk-in cold rooms. Blue Star's other businesses include marketing and maintenance of hi-tech electronic and industrial products such as Testing Machines, Data Communication products, Medical and Analytical Instruments and Special Control Valves.

The Blue Star lines of business include Central Air-conditioning, Room Air-condoners, Commercial Refrigeration, Commercial Equipment, and Professional Electronics and Industrial Products.

Ever since, there has been a constant and profitable growth. Blue Star diversified and took up agencies for Material Testing Machines and Business Machines. The export arena beckoned and the Company began exporting water coolers to Dubai, where in fact, 'Blue Star' soon became the generic name for water coolers.

Strength:

- More than 50 years of experience designing cost effective solution around high-technology products
- Extensive sales and support infrastructure with 29 offices across the country
- Dedicated market development managers with a keen eye for sensing opportunities and establishing a niche
- Ability to attract and retain talent, resulting in a pool of intelligent, qualified and skilled personnel
- Ongoing training and knowledge empowerment activities to provide quality service for equipment promoted by us and effective application support
- Regular presence at related trade shows, to identify channels for future growth
- Investments in creating and maintaining service infrastructure with relevant test equipment and tools for each one of the businesses

Product Portfolio:

Our products are used by organizations which perform physical tests, evaluation and analysis on various materials ranging from Metals to Non-Metals. Our customers are primarily from Quality Control and R&D departments, Testing Labs, Research Labs and Technical institutions all across the country.

- Universal Testing Machines (Electronic, Computerized, Servo Controlled) of Hydraulic as well as Electro-Mechanical Types.

- Hardness Testers (Analog, Digital, Motorized, Computerized) of Micro Vickers, Vickers, Brinell, Rockwell, Portable Types.

- Impact Testers (Analog, Digital, Motorized Pendulum, Fully Computerized) of Charpy, Izod Types for both metals and non-metals.

- Compression Testing Machines, Spring Testing Machines, Rope & Chain Testing Machines

- Dynamic Machines

- Fatigue Testing Machines

- Creep Testing Machines

- Environmental Chambers (Temperature-Humidity, Salt Spray, Rain Simulation, UV, Altitute)

- Plant Growth Chambers

- Drop Weight Testers

- Erichsen Cupping Tester

- Torsion Testing Machines

- Footwear & Leather Testing Machines

- Cable and Wire Testing Machines

- Fiber Optic Cable Testing Machines

- Textile & Paper Testing Machines

- Motorcycle & Bicycle Testing Machines

CHAPTER 5

ANALYSIS OF PROFITABILITY

1. PROFITABILITY ANALYSIS OF THE SELECTED ELECTRONICS INDUSTRY

    A. ANALYSIS OF PROFITABILITY FROM THE VIEW POINT OF FINANICAL MANAGEMENT

        1. OPERATING PROTIF RATIO

        2. GROSS PROFIT RATIO

        3. RETURN ON CAPITAL EMPLOYED

    B. ANALYSIS OF PROFITABILITY FROM THE VIEW POINT OF SHAREHOLDERS

        1. NET PROFIT RATIO

        2. RETURN ON NET WORTH

        3. DIVIDEND PAYOUT RATIO

        4. EARNING PER SHAR

1. PROFITABILITY ANALYSIS OF THE SELECTED ELECTRONICS INDUSTRY

The profitability of Electronics Industry in India has been analyses from the point of view Financial Management and Shareholders. Profitability can be measured in terms of different components of profit and loss account and balance sheet.

A. Analysis of the profitability from the view point of Financial Management

A financial manager is very much interested to locate and pin-point the cause which are responsible for low or high profitability. The financial manager should continuously evaluate the efficiency of its company in terms of profit. In analyzing the profitability of electronics industry in India, the following ratios are considered.

1. **Operating Profit Ratio**
2. **Gross Profit Ratio**
3. **Return on Capital Employed**

1. Operating Profit Ratio:

Return on sales (ROS) is a ratio widely used to evaluate an entity's operating performance. It is also known as "**operating profit margin**" or "**operating margin**". ROS indicates how much profit an entity makes after paying for variable costs of production such as wages, raw materials, etc. (but before interest and tax). It is the return achieved from standard operations and does not include unique or one off transactions. ROS is usually expressed as a percentage of sales (revenue).

$$\text{Operating Profit Ratio} = \frac{\text{Operating Profit}}{\text{Net Sales}} \times 100$$

Return on sales (operating margin) can be used both as a tool to analyze a single company's performance against its past performance, and to compare similar companies' performances against one another. The ratio varies widely by industry but is useful for comparing different companies in the same business. As with many ratios, it is best to compare a company's ROS over time to look for trends, and compare it to other companies in the industry. An increasing ROS indicates the company is becoming more efficient, while a decreasing ratio could signal looming financial troubles. Though, in some instances, a low return on sales can be offset by increased sales.

Table No. 1

Operating Profit Ratio of Selected Electronics Industry in India

(From 2003-04 to 2012-13)

(In Percentage)

Year	BEL	CEL	MEL	TEL	BSL	Average
2003-04	18.2	30.79	7.46	4.33	6.18	13.392
2004-05	21.11	25.97	6.21	5.21	6.39	12.978
2005-06	24.32	19.33	6.74	3.33	7.48	12.24
2006-07	24.25	18.62	5.89	4.47	7.08	12.062
2007-08	24.59	26.17	5.64	1.59	10.07	13.612
2008-09	23.88	12.37	3.81	0.07	10.34	10.094
2009-10	16.91	6.56	3.92	1.55	10.97	7.982
2010-11	16.59	8.73	3.86	4.98	8.68	8.568
2011-12	10.75	10.25	1.15	4.38	-0.37	5.232
2012-13	10.57	0.65	0.34	3.52	3.57	3.73
Average	19.117	15.944	4.502	3.343	7.039	9.989

Source: Computed from Published Annual Reports of the respective Electronics Companies.

Chart No. 1

Operating Profit Ratio of Selected Electronics Industry in India

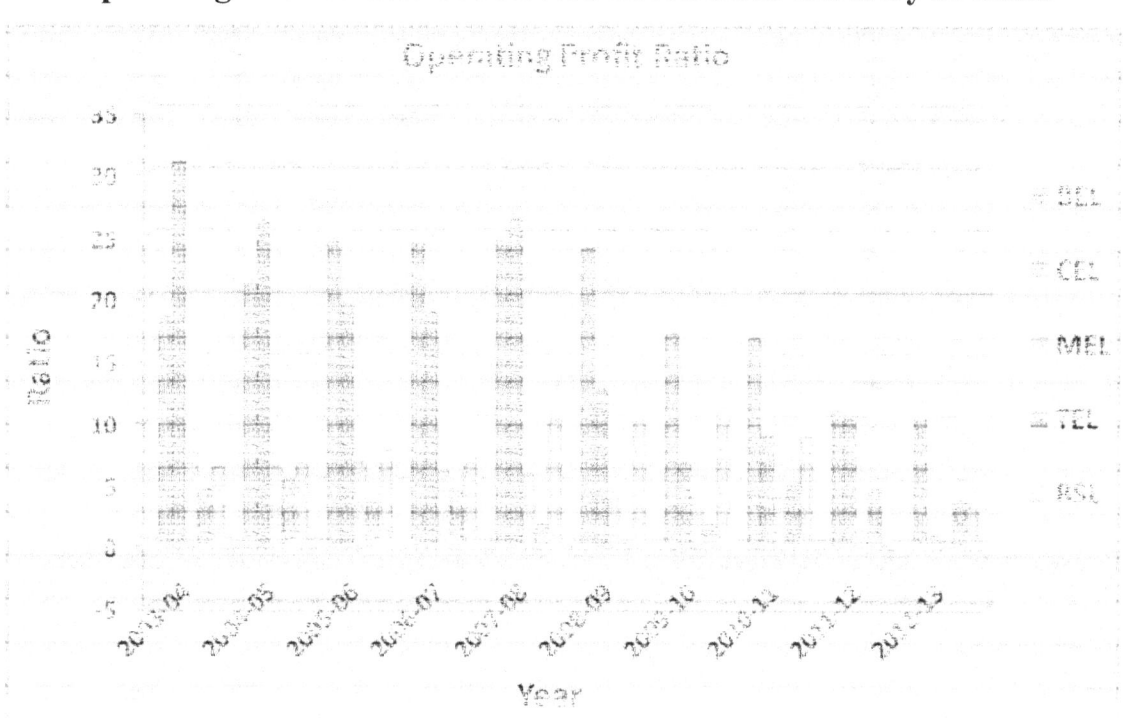

Bharat Electronics Ltd.

Table no.1 the Operating Profit Ratio of BEL Company recorded a fluctuating trend during the study period. Increasing ratio it was 18.20 per cent in 2003-04 and 24.59 per cent in 2007-08. Than after continuously decreasing ratio it was 23.88 per cent in 2008-09 and 10.57 per cent in 2012-13. The average operating profit ratio was 19.117 per cent this company was topper in all the companies. It can be concluded that the performance of this company was satisfactory.

Centum Electronics Ltd.

Table no.1 the Operating Profit Ratio of CEL Company recorded a fluctuating trend during the study period. Decreasing ratio it was 30.79 per cent in 2003-04 and 18.62 per cent in 2006-07. Then after increasing ratio it was 26.17 per cent in 2007-08 and then fluctuating trend in study period. The highest ratio was

30.79 per cent in 2003-04 and the lowest ratio was 0.65 per cent in 2012-13. The average of operating profit ratio was 15.944 per cent.

MIRC Electronics Ltd.

Table no.1 the Operating Profit Ratio of MEL Company recorded fluctuating trend during the study period. Decreasing ratio it was 7.46 per cent in 2003-04 and 6.21 per cent in 2004-05. Then after increasing ratio it was 6.74 per cent in 2005-06 and then decreasing ratio it was 5.89 per cent in 2006-07 and 3.81 per cent in 2008-09. The highest ratio was 7.46 per cent in 2003-04 and the lowest ratio was in 0.34 per cent in 2012-13. The average operating profit ratio was 4.502 per cent.

TVS Electronics Ltd.

Table no.1 the Operating Profit Ratio of TEL Company recorded a fluctuating trend during the study period. Increasing ratio it was 4.33 in 2003-04 and 5.21 in 2004-05 then after decreasing ratio in study period. The ratio was the highest of 5.21 in 2004-05 and the lowest was 0.07 in 2007-08. The average operating profit ratio was 3.343. It can be concluded that the performance of this company was satisfactory.

Blue Stare Ltd.

Table no.1 the Operating Profit Ratio of BSL Company recorded a fluctuating trend during the study period. Increasing ratio it was 6.18 per cent in 2003-04 and 7.48 per cent in 2005-06 and then decreasing ratio it was 7.08 in 2006-07. The highest ratio was 10.97 per cent in 2009-10 and the lowest ratio was negative (- 0.37) per cent in 2011-12. The average operating profit ratio was 7.039 per cent. The reason for it was high inputs cost and decreasing selling price. On the whole, the performance of BEL and CE were better than MIRC, TVS and BSL.

F- Test (ANOVA):

Null Hypothesis: There is no any significance difference in operating profit ratio of selected Electronics Companies in India.

Alternative Hypothesis: There is significance difference in operating profit ratio of selected Electronics Companies in India.

For testing these hypothesis one way ANOVA test has been used as shown in table as below.

Table No. 2

F-Test (ANOVA) of Operating Profit Ratio

Source of Variation	SS	d.f.	MS	F Value	F crit (5%)
Between Groups	2017.61	4	504.4035	17.3107	2.5787
Within Groups	1311.224	45	29.13832		
Total	3328.838	49			

The analysis showed the significance result. It can be seen from the table, that the calculated value of 'F' was found as 17.3107 while the table value of 'F' was 2.5787 at 5% level of significance. The calculated value of 'F' being greater than the table value 'F', the null hypothesis stood rejected and the alternative hypothesis accepted at 5% level of significance.

2. Gross Profit Ratio:

This ratio expresses the relationship of gross profit to sales, in term of percentage. The determinate of this ratio are the gross profit and sales. This ratio is of vital importance for gauzing raging business results. A low gross profit ratio will suggest decline in business, which may be to insufficient sales, higher cost of production with the exiting or reduced selling price or the all-round inefficient management. The financial management must be able to detect the causes of a falling gross profit ratio and initiate action to improve the situation. The higher gross profit is a sign of good efficient management it is calculated as follows:

$$\text{Gross Profit Ratio} = \frac{\text{Gross Profit}}{\text{Sales}} \times 100$$

Gross profit margin (gross margin) is the ratio of gross profit (gross sales less cost of sales) to sales revenue. It is the percentage by which gross profits exceed production costs. Gross margins reveal how much a company earns taking into consideration the costs that it incurs for producing its products or services. Gross margin is a good indication of how profitable a company is at the most fundamental level, how efficiently a company uses its resources, materials, and labor. It is usually expressed as a percentage, and indicates the profitability of a business before overhead costs; it is a measure of how well a company controls its costs.

Table No. 3

Gross Profit Ratio of Selected Electronics Industry in India

(From 2003-04 to 2012-13)

(In Percentage)

Year	BEL	CEL	MEL	TEL	BSL	Average
2003-04	15.83	30.73	5.42	3.74	7.17	12.578
2004-05	18.77	27.65	4.25	4.09	6.89	12.33
2005-06	21.88	19.67	4.70	3.20	7.55	11.4
2006-07	21.95	16.48	4.41	1.89	7.03	10.352
2007-08	22.20	21.30	3.90	-0.91	9.08	11.114
2008-09	21.51	3.39	2.35	-2.42	9.32	6.83

2009-10	14.64	-0.45	2.48	-0.80	9.60	5.094
2010-11	14.34	4.77	2.63	2.79	7.57	6.42
2011-12	8.63	6.13	-0.22	2.05	-1.53	3.012
2012-13	8.39	-3.54	-0.98	0.89	2.39	1.43
Average	16.814	12.613	2.894	1.452	6.507	8.056

Source: Computed from Published Annual Reports of the respective Electronics Companies.

Chart No. 2

Gross Profit Ratio of Selected Electronics Industry in India

Bharat Electronics Ltd.

Table no.3 the Gross Profit Ratio of BEL Company indicated a fluctuating trend during the study period. Increasing ratio it was 15.83 per cent in 2003-04 and 22.20 per cent in 2007-08. Than after continuously decreasing ratio it was 21.51 per cent in 2008-09 and 8.39 per cent in 2012-13. The highest ratio was 22.20 per cent in 2007-08 and the lowest ratio was 8.39 per cent in 2012-13. The average of gross profit ratio was 16.814 per cent which was also higher as compared to all companies under the study.

Centum Electronics Ltd.

Table no.3 the Gross Profit Ratio of CEL Company indicated a fluctuating trend during the study period. Decreasing ratio it was 30.73 per cent in 2003-04 and 16.48 per cent in 2006-07. Then after increasing ratio it was 21.30 per cent in 2007-08 and then fluctuating trend in study period. The highest ratio was 30.73 per cent in 2003-04 and the lowest ratio was negative (-3.54) per cent in 2012-13. The average of gross profit ratio was 12.613 per cent.

MIRC Electronics Ltd.

Table no.3 the Gross Profit Ratio of MEL Company indicated a fluctuating trend during the study period. Decreasing ratio it was 5.42 per cent in 2003-04 and 4.25 per cent in 2004-05 and then after fluctuating trend in study period. The highest ratio was 5.42 per cent in 2003-04 and the lowest ratio was negative (-0.98) in 2012-13. The average of gross profit ratio was 2.894 per cent.

TVS Electronics Ltd.

Table no.3 the Gross Profit Ratio of TEL Company indicated a fluctuating trend during the study period. Increasing ratio it was 3.74 per cent in 2003-04 and 4.09 per cent in 2004-05 then after decreasing ratio was negative (-2.42) per cent in 2008-09. The highest ratio was 4.09 in 2004-05 and the lowest ratio was negative (-2.42) in 2007-08. The average gross profit ratio was 1.452 per cent

Blue Stare Ltd.

Table no.3 the Gross Profit Ratio of BSL Company indicated a fluctuating trend during the study period. Decreasing ratio it was 7.17 per cent in 2003-04 and 6.89 per cent in 2005-06 and then after fluctuating trend in study period. The highest ratio was 9.60 per cent in 2009-10 and the lowest ratio was negative (-1.53) in 2011-12. The average of gross profit ratio was 6.507 per cent.

From the above point of performance of Bharat Electronics Ltd. was better as compared to other Companies.

F- Test (ANOVA):

Null Hypothesis: There is no any significance difference in gross profit ratio of selected Electronics Companies in India.

Alternative Hypothesis: There is significance difference in gross profit ratio of selected Electronics Companies in India.

For testing these hypothesis one way ANOVA test has been used as shown in table as below.

Table No. 4

F-Test (ANOVA) of Gross Profit Ratio

Source of Variation	SS	d.f.	MS	F Value	F crit (5%)
Between Groups	1701.273	4	425.3182	10.8517	2.5787
Within Groups	1763.712	45	39.1936		
Total	3464.985	49			

The analysis showed the significance result. It can be seen from the table, that the calculated value of 'F' was found as 10.8517 while the table value of 'F' was 2.5787 at 5% level of significance. The calculated value of 'F' being greater than the table value 'F', the null hypothesis stood rejected and the alternative hypothesis accepted at 5% level of significance.

3. Return on Capital Employed:

The primary objective of making investment in any business is to obtain adequate return on capital invested. Therefore, to measure the overall profitability of the bank, it is essential to compare operating profit with capital employed. It is also called "Return on Investment" (ROI) In relation to banking sector return on capital employed is an important ratio for measuring the efficiency of management in utilization of funds supplied by depositors and owners. It expresses profitability on overall investment viz. total resources utilized by the bank. The capital employed is equal to owner's funds plus long-term deposits. Thus capital employed basis provide a test of profitability related to the long-term funds. The formula used is as follows:

$$\text{Return on Capital Employed Ratio} = \frac{\text{Net Profit}}{\text{Capital Employed}} \times 100$$

Net Profit = Profit after tax.

Capital Employed = Owners funds plus long- term deposits.

The higher the ratio, more efficiency of the management in utilizing funds entrusted to them and better is the financial position of bank. This ratio indicates the earning power of the bank on each rupee invested. This ratio is useful for management to take investment decisions in form of deposits in a particular bank and judging the prospects or stability of the bank.

Table No. 5

Return on Capital Employed of Selected Electronics Industry in India

(From 2003-04 to 2012-13)

(In Percentage)

Year	BEL	CEL	MEL	TEL	BSL	Average
2003-04	40.15	30.37	19.27	11.79	29.56	26.228
2004-05	42.84	25.88	12.74	12.18	29.34	24.596
2005-06	42.08	26.77	16.70	6.49	31.63	24.734
2006-07	39.67	41.58	18.60	7.70	33.58	28.226
2007-08	34.19	30.45	14.70	6.53	69.82	31.138
2008-09	30.84	5.14	8.16	0.06	64.09	21.658
2009-10	22.25	0.55	10.99	2.16	50.35	17.26
2010-11	21.57	8.72	13.37	7.77	22.71	14.828
2011-12	18.75	10.68	-0.23	7.54	-4.15	6.518
2012-13	17.33	-4.29	-3.41	4.62	11.81	5.212
Average	30.967	17.585	11.089	6.684	33.874	20.04

Source: Computed from Published Annual Reports of the respective Electronics Companies

Chart No. 3

Return on Capital Employed of Selected Electronics Industry in India

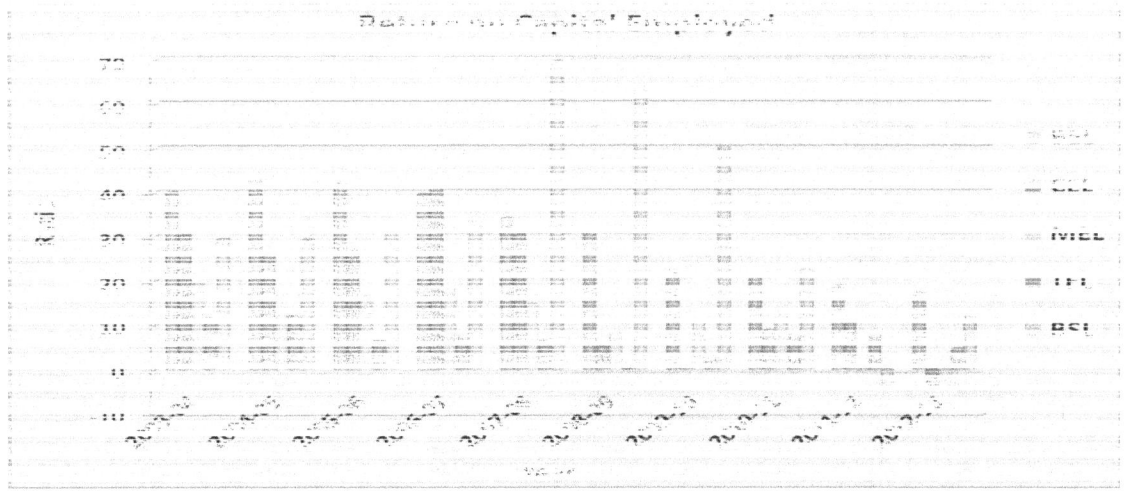

Bharat Electronics Ltd.

Table no.7 showed the Return on Capital Employed of BEL Company a decreasing trend during the study period. Increasing ratio it was 40.15 per cent in 2003-04 and 42.84 per cent in 2004-05, then after continuously decreasing trend in study period. The highest ratio was 42.84 per cent in 2004-05 and the lowest ratio was 17.33 per cent in 2012-13. The average rate of return on capital employed was 30.967 per cent above the total average of industry and the overall financial efficiency has been good.

Centum Electronics Ltd.

Table no.7 the Return on Capital Employed of CEL Company recorded a very fluctuating trend during the study period. Decreasing ratio it was 30.37 per cent in 2003-04 and 25.88 per cent in 2004-05 and then after fluctuating trend in study period. The highest ratio was 41.58 per cent in 2006-07 and the lowest ratio was negative (-4.29) per cent in 2012-13. The average of return on capital employed was 17.585 per cent.

MIRC Electronics Ltd.

Table no.7 the Return on Capital Employed of MEL Company indicated a fluctuating ratio during the study period. Decreasing ratio it was 19.27 per cent in 2003-04 and 12.74 in 2004-05 and then after fluctuating trend in study period. The highest ratio was 19.27 in 2003-04 and the lowest was in negative (-3.41) in 2012-13. The average rate of return on capital employed was 11.089 per cent which was lower than industry average rate.

TVS Electronics Ltd.

Table no.7 the Return on Capital Employed of TEL Company recorded a fluctuating trend during the study period. Increasing ratio it was 11.79 per cent in

2003-04 and 12.18 per cent in 2004-05 then after fluctuating trend in study period. The highest ratio was 12.18 per cent in 2004-05 and the lowest ratio was 0.06 per cent in 2008-09. The average rate of return on capital employed was 6.684 per cent which was lowest rate of among all the companies under study.

Blue Stare Ltd.

Table no.7 the Return on Capital Employed of BSL Company recorded a fluctuating trend during the study period. Decreasing ratio it was 29.56 per cent in 2003-04 and 29.34 per cent in 2004-05 and then after fluctuating trend in study period. The highest ratio was 69.82 per cent in 2007-08 and the lowest ratio was negative (- 4.15) per cent in 2011-12. The average rate of return on capital employed was 33.874 per cent which was higher rate of among all the companies under study. It indicated satisfactory rate of return on capital employed.

F- Test (ANOVA):

Null Hypothesis: There is no any significance difference in return on capital employed of selected Electronics Companies in India.

Alternative Hypothesis: There is significance difference in return on capital employed of selected Electronics Companies in India.

For testing these hypothesis one way ANOVA test has been used as shown in table as below.

Table No. 6
F-Test (ANOVA) of Return on Capital Employed

Source of Variation	SS	d.f.	MS	F Value	F crit (5%)
Between Groups	5753.09	4	1438.273	7.8252	2.5787
Within Groups	8270.96	45	183.7992		
Total	14024.05	49			

The analysis showed the significant result. It can be seen from the table, that the calculated value of 'F' was found as 7.8252 while the table value of 'F' was 2.5787 at 5% level of significance. The calculated value of 'F' being greater than the table value 'F', the null hypothesis stood rejected and the alternative hypothesis accepted at 5% level of significance.

B. ANALYSIS OF THE PROFITABILITY FROM THE VIEW POINT OF SHAREHOLDER'S:

The owners, the shareholders have permanent stake in the enterprise and as such they have to share the prosperity marked by higher profitability and adversity marked by losses. The financial welfare of the owners increases when net profit after tax has increase and also when they receive large share of dividend. For this analysis, following ratios are calculated.

1. **Net Profit Ratio**
2. **Return on Net Worth**
3. **Earning Per Share**
4. **Dividend Pay-out Ratio**

1.   Net Profit Ratio:

As pointed out by Hingorani, Ramanathan and Grewal, "Net profit margin indicates the net margin earned in a sale of Rs. 100." Vam Home states that net profit "Tells us the relative efficiency of the firm after taking into account all expenses and income taxes, but not extra –ordinary charges." Net Profit is obtained after deducting amount of operating expenses, interest and taxes from the gross profit amount. Net profit after taxes is nothing but the sum of dividends (paid or provided for) plus the retained earnings. Net profit ratio is measured by dividing net profit after taxes by sales. Thus,

$$\text{Net Profit Ratio} = \frac{\text{Net Profit}}{\text{Net Sales}} \times 100$$

Again no specific norm has set for measurement of net profit margin ratio. If the ratio is shows as increasing trend year after year. It may be concluded that business conditions are improving. Talking of an exception, a company with a low profit margin can earn a high rate of return on investment. This can happen only if the company has higher inventory turnover. Moreover, if net profit margin ratio is interpreted with gross profit margin ratio jointly, it adds meaning to the firm's profitability.

"A high net profit margin would ensure adequate return to the owners as

well as enable a firm to withstand adverse economic conditions when the selling price is declining, cost of production is rising and demand for the product is falling." The inadequate net profit would debar the company from paying off its debts and giving a satisfactory return to its shareholders. "This ratio indicates a firm's capacity to withstand adverse conditions which may arise because of various reasons such as; (1) falling price, (2) rising cost, and (3) declining sales." In simple words, a firm having net margin ratio would be benefited in terms of better surviving conditions in the times of falling selling prices, rising cost of production or declining demand for the production.

Table No. 7
Net Profit Ratio of Selected Electronics Industry in India
(From 2003-04 to 2012-13)

(In Percentage)

Year	BEL	CEL	MEL	TEL	BSL	Average
2003-04	11.11	23.35	4.67	1.36	4.61	9.02
2004-05	13.20	29.78	2.07	1.25	4.23	10.106
2005-06	15.90	11.77	2.13	1.18	4.14	7.024
2006-07	17.27	12.54	2.34	0.66	4.43	7.448
2007-08	18.92	13.19	2.29	5.91	7.80	9.622
2008-09	15.23	1.63	0.54	-3.22	7.02	4.24
2009-10	13.19	-0.28	1.30	-2.50	8.34	4.01
2010-11	14.77	1.80	1.49	0.84	5.40	4.86
2011-12	13.00	2.86	-2.30	0.63	-3.29	2.18
2012-13	13.20	-3.15	-2.38	-3.36	1.84	1.23
Average	14.579	9.349	1.215	0.275	4.452	5.974

Source: Computed from Published Annual Reports of the respective Electronics Companies.

Chart No. 4

Net Profit Ratio of Selected Electronics Industry in India

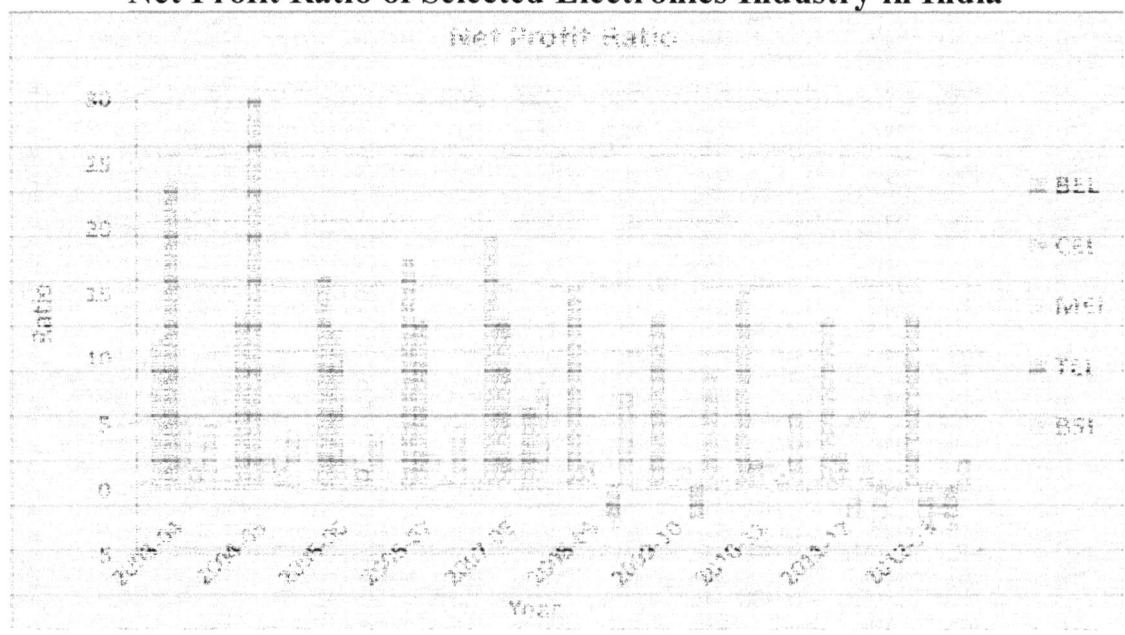

Bharat Electronics Ltd.

Table no.5 the Net Profit Ratio of BEL Company recorded a fluctuating trend during the study period. Increasing ratio it was 11.11 per cent in 2003-04 and 18.92 per cent in 2007-08. And then after continuously is fluctuating trend in study period. The highest ratio was 18.92 per cent in 2007-08 and the lowest ratio was 11.11 per cent in 2012-13. The average of net profit ratio was 14.579 per cent which was also higher as compared to all companies under the study.

Centum Electronics Ltd.

Table no.5 the Net Profit Ratio of CEL Company recorded a fluctuating trend during the study period. Increasing ratio it was 23.35 per cent in 2003-04 and 29.78 per cent in 2004-05. Then after decreasing ratio it was 11.77 per cent in 2005-06 and negative (-0.28) then after fluctuating ratio in study period. The highest ratio was 29.78 per cent in 2004-05 and the lowest ratio was negative (-3.15) in 2012-13. The average of net profit ratio was 9.349 per cent. Performance of this company considerably was satisfactory in first five years of study period as compared to its last five years of study period.

MIRC Electronics Ltd.

Table no.5 the Net Profit Ratio of MEL Company recorded a fluctuating trend during the study period. Decreasing ratio it was 4.67 per cent in 2003-04 and 2.07 per cent in 2004-05 and then after fluctuating trend in study period. The highest ratio was 4.67 per cent in 2003-04 and the lowest ratio was in -2.38 in 2012-13. The average of net profit ratio was 1.215 per cent.

TVS Electronics Ltd.

Table no.5 showed the Net Profit Ratio of TEL Company with the fluctuating trend during the study period. Decreasing ratio it was 1.36 per cent in 2003-04 and 0.66 per cent in 2006-07 then after fluctuating trend in study period. The highest ratio was 5.91 per cent in 2007-08 and the lowest ratio was negative (-3.36) per cent in 2012-13. The average of net profit ratio was 0.275 per cent. The average ratio of this indicates that the position of net profit ratio was very worst. The TVS should take necessary action to improve the position.

Blue Stare Ltd.

Table no.5 the Net Profit Ratio of BSL Company recorded a fluctuating trend during the study period. Decreasing ratio it was 4.61 per cent in 2003-04 and 4.14 per cent in 2006-07 and then after fluctuating trend in study period. The highest ratio was 8.34 per cent in 2009-10 and the lowest ratio was negative (-3.29) in 2011-12. The average of net profit ratio was 4.452 per cent.

Thus, it can be concluded the net profit ratio of BEL and CE were satisfactory but in MIRC, TVS and BSL it was not up to work in companies due to external factors.

F- Test (ANOVA):

Null Hypothesis: There is no any significance difference in net profit ratio of selected Electronics Companies in India.

Alternative Hypothesis: There is significance difference in net profit ratio of selected Electronics Companies in India.

For testing these hypothesis one way ANOVA test has been used as shown in table as below.

Table No. 8

F-Test (ANOVA) of Net Profit Ratio

Source of Variation	SS	d.f.	MS	F Value	F crit (5%)
Between Groups	1428.798	4	357.1995	12.2577	2.5787
Within Groups	1311.341	45	29.1409		
Total	2740.139	49			

The analysis showed the significance result. It can be seen from the table, that the calculated value of 'F' was found as 12.2577 while the table value of 'F' was 2.5787 at 5% level of significance. The calculated value of 'F' being greater than the table value 'F', the null hypothesis stood rejected and the alternative hypothesis accepted at 5% level of significance.

2. Return on Net Worth / Shareholders Equity:

One of the objectives of operating a company is to seek benefit of its shareholders. Shareholders are all the more interested in knowing the amount of return entitled to them by the company on the investment made by them. Return on shareholders' equity calculates the profitability of owner's investment. So, the formula derived is:

$$\text{Return on Net Worth} = \frac{\text{Net Profit after Intrest and Taxes}}{\text{Total Shareholders' Equity}} \times 100$$

This ratio is expressed in terms of percentage of net profit (after interest and taxes) earn on owner's equity. Shareholder's equity includes equity share capital, preference share capital, share premium, reserve and other funds. Anthony and Reece are of the opinion that this ratio "Reflect that how much the firm has earned on the funds invested by the shareholders." "Thus, this ratio is of great interest to the present as well as prospective shareholders and also of great concern to management." As it significantly tells how efficiently the firm is using the resources of the owners i.e. the shareholders of the company.

Table No. 9

Return on Net Worth of Selected Electronics Industry in India

(From 2003-04 to 2012-13)

(In Percentage)

Year	BEL	CEL	MEL	TEL	BSL	Average
2003-04	25.27	38.20	23.33	9.91	25.01	24.344
2004-05	27.32	35.51	12.26	10.13	26.32	22.308
2005-06	28.14	21.69	13.05	7.70	28.26	19.768
2006-07	27.19	45.43	15.98	4.48	33.37	25.29
2007-08	25.05	20.36	14.50	25.24	66.32	30.294
2008-09	19.20	1.14	3.07	-14.71	49.13	11.566
2009-10	16.46	-0.43	7.85	-12.32	43.01	10.914
2010-11	17.04	4.31	11.13	3.77	27.02	12.654
2011-12	14.34	6.35	-17.45	3.29	-18.18	-2.33
2012-13	13.70	-7.52	-16.32	-23.33	10.46	-4.602
Average	21.371	16.504	6.74	1.416	29.072	15.021

Source: Computed from Published Annual Reports of the respective Electronics Companies.

Chart No. 5
Return on Net Worth of Selected Electronics Industry in India

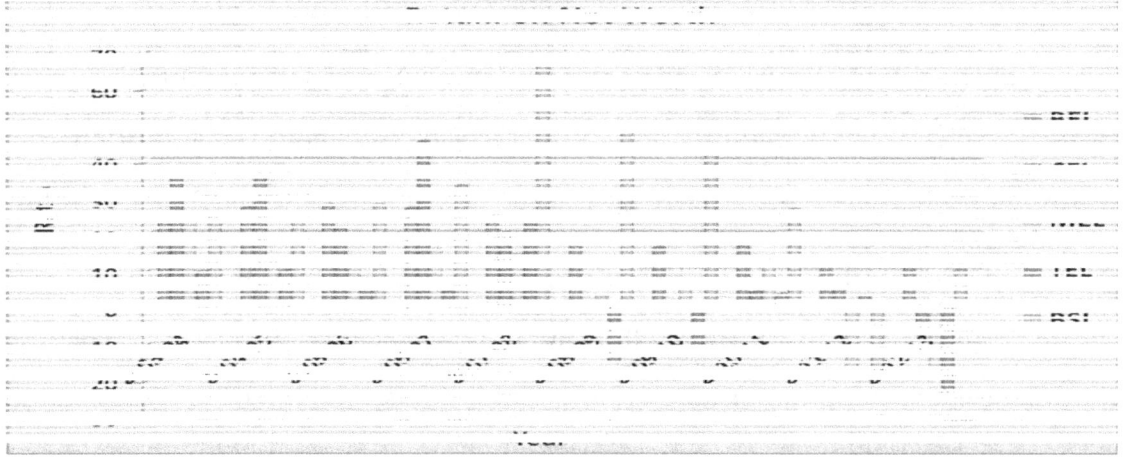

Bharat Electronics Ltd.

Table no.9 the Return on Net Worth of BEL Company recorded a fluctuating trend during the study period. Increasing ratio it was 25.27 per cent in 2003-04 and 28.14 per cent in 2005-06. Decreasing ratio it was 27.19 per cent in 2006-07 and 16.46 per cent in 2009-10, then after continuously fluctuating trend in study period. The highest ratio was 28.14 per cent in 2005-06 and the lowest ratio was 13.70 per cent in 2012-13. The average rate of return on net worth was 21.371 per cent.

Centum Electronics Ltd.

Table no.9 the Return on Net Worth Ratio of CEL Company indicated a fluctuating trend during the study period. Decreasing ratio it was 38.20 per cent in 2003-04 and 21.69 per cent in 2005-06, then after fluctuating trend in study period. The highest ratio was 45.43 per cent in 2006-07 and the lowest ratio was negative (-7.52) in 2012-13. The average rate of return on net worth was 16.504 per cent.

MIRC Electronics Ltd.

Table no.9 the Return on Net Worth of MEL Company recorded a fluctuating trend during the study period. Decreasing ratio it was 23.33 per cent in 2003-04 and 12.26 per cent in 2004-05. Increasing ratio it was 15.98 in 2006-07, then after fluctuating trend in study period. The highest ratio was 23.33 per cent in 2003-04 and the lowest ratio was negative (-17.45) in 2011-12, it indicated loss. The average rate of return on net worth was 6.74 per cent which was lowest in industry average.

TVS Electronics Ltd.

Table no.9 the Return on Net Worth of TEL Company recorded a fluctuating trend during the study period. Increasing ratio it was 9.91 per cent in 2003-04 and

10.13 per cent in 2004-05, then after fluctuating trend in study period. The highest ratio was 25.24 per cent in 2007-08 and the lowest ratio was negative (-23.33) per cent in 2012-13, it indicated loss. The average rate of return on net worth was 1.416 per cent.

Blue Stare Ltd.

Table no.9 the Return on Net Worth of BSL Company recorded a fluctuating trend during the study period. Increasing ratio it was 25.01 per cent in 2003-04 and 66.32 per cent in 2007-08. Decreasing ratio it was 49.13 per cent in 2008-09 and negative (-18.18) in 2011-12. The highest ratio was 66.32 per cent in 2007-08 and the lowest ratio was (-18.18) per cent in 2011-12. The average rate of return on net worth was 29.072 per cent which was highest among all the companies under study.

On the basis of the above analysis it can be concluded that the performance of BSL was highly satisfactory because of its average rate of return on owner's equity was 29.072 per cent which were highest industry average. BEL and CEL were higher than the industry average. MEL and TEL to improve the rate of return on shareholders' equity, it is suggested that the units of Electronics industry under the study should maintain a low capital gearing ratio by reducing the amount of debt capital.

F - Test (ANOVA):

Null Hypothesis: There is no any significance difference in return on net worth of selected Electronics Companies in India.

Alternative Hypothesis: There is significance difference in return on net worth of selected Electronics Companies in India.

For testing these hypothesis one way ANOVA test has been used as shown in table as below.

Table No. 10

F-Test (ANOVA) of Return on Net Worth

Source of Variation	SS	d.f.	MS	F Value	F crit (5%)
Between Groups	4936.234	4	1234.058	4.8504	2.5787
Within Groups	11449.13	45	254.425		
Total	16385.36	49			

The analysis showed the significance result. It can be seen from the table, that the calculated value of 'F' was found as 4.8504 while the table value of 'F' was 2.5787 at 5% level of significance. The calculated value of 'F' being greater than the table value 'F', the null hypothesis stood rejected and the alternative hypothesis accepted at 5% level of significance.

3. Earning Per Share:

Earning per share (EPS) is the portion of the company's distributable profit which is allocated to each outstanding equity share (common share). Earning per share is a very good indicator of the profitability of any organization, and it is one of the most widely used measures of profitability, and when compared with EPS of other similar companies, it gives a view of the comparative earning power of the companies. EPS when calculated over a number of years indicates whether the earning power of the company has improved or deteriorated. Investors usually look for companies with steadily increasing earnings per share.

Growth in EPS is an important measure of management performance because it shows how much money the company is making for its shareholders, not only due to changes in profit, but also after all the effects of issuance of new shares (this is especially important when the growth comes as a result of acquisition). This can be expressed in terms of the following formula:

$$\text{Earnings Per Share} = \frac{\text{Net Profit} - \text{Preference Dividend}}{\text{Number of Equity Shares}}$$

It should be noted that two different companies could generate the same EPS but one could do so with a lesser equity. All other things being equal, this company is better than the other one because it is more efficient at using its capital for generating profits. It is important that the investors do not rely on only measure of earnings per share for making investment decisions.

Table No. 11

Earning Per Share of Selected Electronics Industry in India

(From 2003-04 to 2012-13)

(In Rupees)

Year	BEL	CEL	MEL	TEL	BSL	Average
2003-04	41.29	5.56	3.11	2.08	18.10	14.028
2004-05	68.81	8.75	1.66	2.27	21.77	20.652
2005-06	74.86	6.70	1.87	1.79	27.19	22.482
2006-07	91.52	17.13	2.56	1.05	7.91	24.034
2007-08	104.67	9.02	2.51	7.23	19.36	28.558
2008-09	94.12	0.50	1.09	-3.57	20.05	22.438
2009-10	92.18	-0.42	1.37	-2.75	23.52	22.78
2010-11	109.77	2.74	2.05	0.87	17.23	26.532
2011-12	105.92	4.23	-2.73	0.79	-9.91	19.66
2012-13	113.90	-4.65	-2.20	-4.53	5.75	21.654
Average	89.704	4.956	1.129	0.523	15.097	22.282

Source: Computed from Published Annual Reports of the respective Electronics Companies.

Chart No. 6

Earning Per Share of Selected Electronics Industry in India

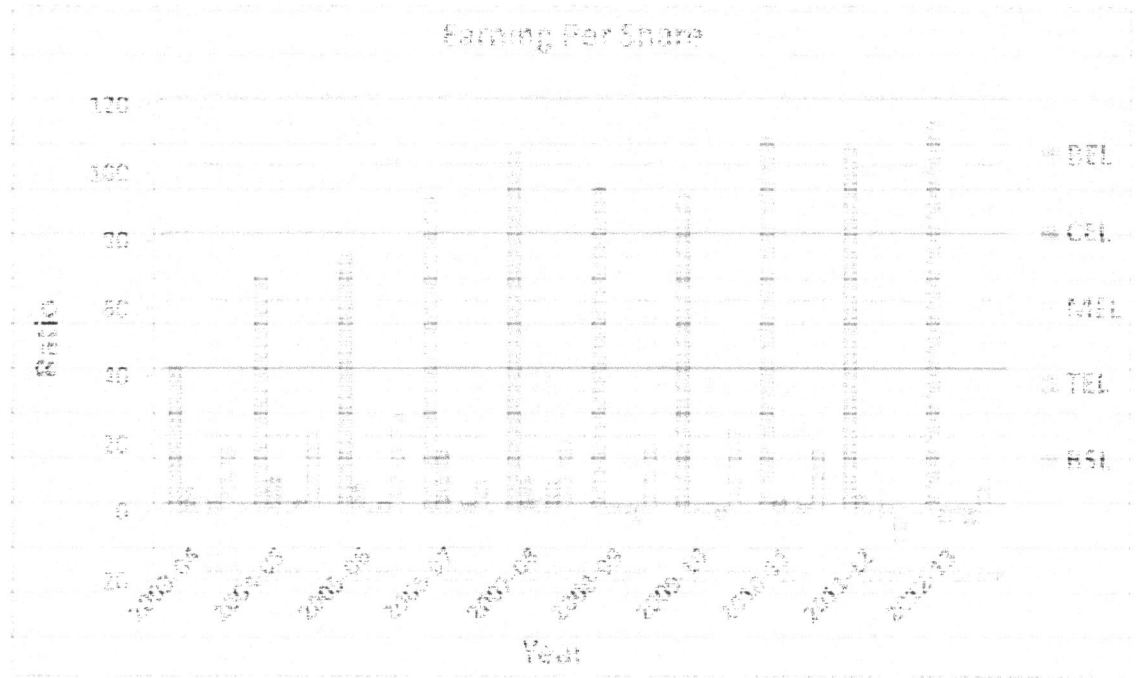

Bharat Electronics Ltd.

Table no.11 the Earning Per Share of BEL Company recorded a fluctuating trend during the study period. It was Rs. 41.29 in 2003-04 and Rs. 104.67 in 2007-08 it showed an increasing trend. Decreasing it was Rs. 94.12 2008-09 and Rs. 92.18 in 2009-10. In 2003-04 it was Rs. 41.29 and reached with Rs.113.90 in 2012-13. The average of earning per share was Rs. 89.704 which was highest among all the companies under study and it was higher than industry average.

Centum Electronics Ltd.

Table no.11 the Earning Per Share of CEL Company recorded a fluctuating trend during the study period. It was Ra. 5.56 in 2003-04 and Rs. 8.75 in 2004-05.

In 2005-06 and 2006-07 it showed an increasing trend. The highest was Rs.17.13 in 2006-07 and the lowest was Rs. negative (-4.65) in 2012-13. Its performance was not up to the mark; because of there was negative EPS in last year of study. The average of earning per share was Rs. 4.956.

MIRC Electronics Ltd.

Table no.11 the Earning Per Share of MEL Company recorded a fluctuating trend during the study period. The earning per share ranged between Rs. (-2.73) in 2011-12 and Rs. 3.11 in 2003-04. The average earning per share was Rs. 1.129 which was lower than industry average. Its performance was not up to the mark; because of there was negative EPS in last two years of study.

TVS Electronics Ltd.

Table no.11 the Earning Per Share of TEL Company recorded a fluctuating trend during the study period. Increasing EPS it was Rs. 2.08 in 2003-04 and Rs. 2.27 in 2004-05. The earning per share ranged between Rs. (-4.53) in 2012-13 and Rs. 7.23 in 2007-08. The average earning per share of this company was Rs. 0.523 which was lower than industry average.

Blue Stare Ltd.

Table no.11 the Earning Per Share of BSL Company recorded a fluctuating trend during the study period. Increasing EPS it was Rs. 18.10 in 2003-04 and Rs. 27.19 in 2005-06, then after fluctuating trend in study period. The highest EPS was Rs. 27.19 in 2005-06 and the lowest was Rs. (-9.91) in 2011-12. The average earning per share was Rs. 15.097 which was highest among all the companies under study.

From the above analysis it can be concluded that low earning per share company should try to increase it by switching over to the owned capital and utilization of borrowed funds, particularly in CEL, MEL and TEL should very much try to increase their earning per share ratio by taking different remedial steps like proper utilization of borrowed funds, better utilization of assets, effective utilization of shareholder's fund, etc.

F-Test (ANOVA):

Null Hypothesis: There is no any significance difference in earning per share of selected Electronics Companies in India.

Alternative Hypothesis: There is significance difference in earning per share of selected Electronics Companies in India.

For testing these hypothesis two way ANOVA test has been used as shown in table as below.

Table No. 12

F-Test (ANOVA) of Earning Per Share

Source of Variation	SS	d.f.	MS	F Value	F crit (5%)
Between Groups	58184.44	4	14546.11	108.0646	2.5787
Within Groups	6057.257	45	134.6057		
Total	64241.7	49			

The analysis showed the significance result. It can be seen from the table, that the calculated value of 'F' was found as 108.0646 while the table value of 'F' was 2.5787 at 5% level of significance. The calculated value of 'F' being greater than the table value 'F', the null hypothesis stood rejected and the alternative hypothesis accepted at 5% level of significance.

4. Dividend Payout Ratio:

Dividend payout ratio compares the dividends paid by a company to its earnings. The relationship between dividends and earnings is important. The part of earnings that is not paid out in dividends is used for reinvestment and growth in future earnings. Investors who are interested in short term earnings prefer to invest in companies with high dividend payout ratio. On the other hand, investors who prefer to have capital growth like to invest in companies with lower dividend payout ratio.

Investors usually seek a consistent and/or improving dividends payout ratio. The dividend payout ratio should not be too high. The earnings should support the payment of dividends. If the company pays high levels of dividends it may become for it to maintain such levels of dividends if the earnings fall in the future. Dividends are paid in cash; therefore, high dividend payout ratio can have implications for the cash management and liquidity of the company.

The formula for calculation of dividend payout ratio is given below:

$$\text{Dividend Payout Ratio} = \frac{\text{Total Dividends}}{\text{Total Net Earnings}} \times 100$$

OR

$$\text{Dividend Payout Ratio} = \frac{\text{Dividend Per Share}}{\text{Earning Per Share}} \times 100$$

It should be noted that the dividends are not paid from "earnings"; in fact they are paid from the "cash". Dividend payout ratio compares dividends to the earnings, not to the cash. A company will not be able to pay dividends if it does not have sufficient cash even if it has a high level of earnings.

Table No. 13

Dividend Payout Ratio of Selected Electronics Industry in India

(From 2003-04 to 2012-13)

(In Percentage)

Year	BEL	CEL	MEL	TEL	BSL	Average
2003-04	27.43	8.5	36.22	40.73	56.1	33.796
2004-05	22.54	9.69	34.96	45.27	52.48	32.988
2005-06	22.25	16.02	37.03	47.64	50.32	34.652
2006-07	22.94	23.34	35.59	83.48	43.44	41.758
2007-08	23.14	12.97	48.03	16.17	42.3	28.522
2008-09	23.29	-	83.01	-	40.85	29.43
2009-10	24.37	-	88.63	-	39.67	30.534
2010-11	22.94	28.95	60.36	-	47.2	31.802
2011-12	22.88	19.98	-	-	-	8.572
2012-13	22.92	-	-	-	52.14	15.012
Average	23.47	11.901	42.383	23.329	42.45	28.7066

Source: Computed from Published Annual Reports of the respective Electronics Companies.

Chart No. 7

Dividend Payout Ratio of Selected Electronics Industry in India

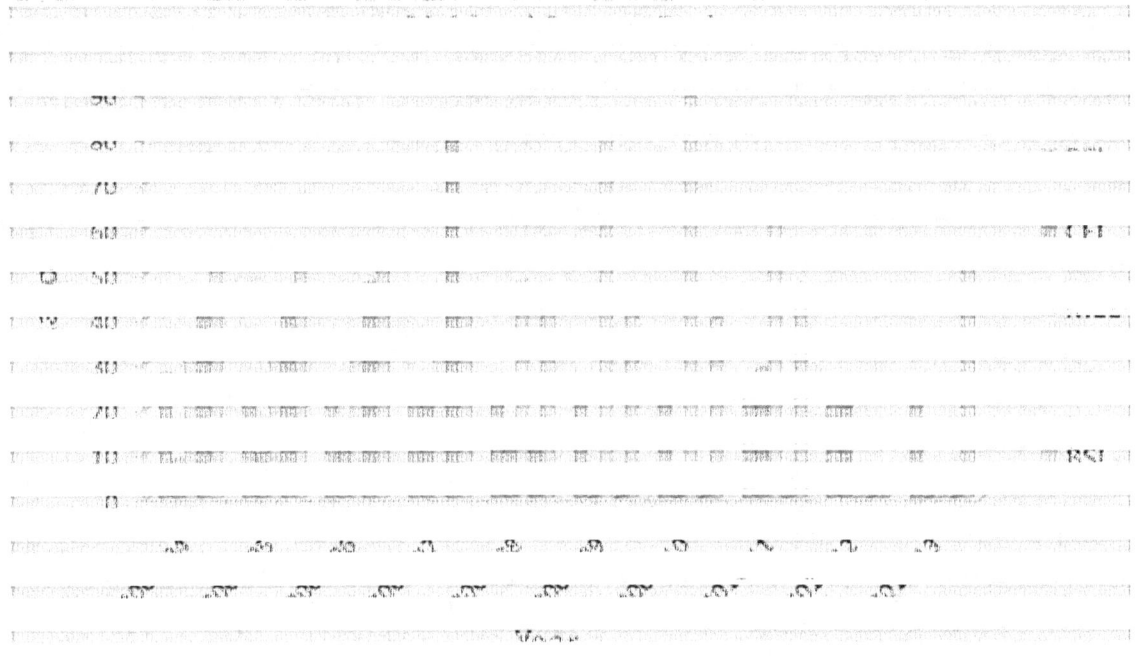

Bharat Electronics Ltd.

Table no.13 clearly indicates that dividend pay-out ratio in BEL Company witnessed a decreasing trend in first three years of study period. It was 27.43 per cent in 2003-04 and 22.25 per cent in 2005-06. In 2006-07 it slight increased and reached 24.37 per cent in 2009-10 then after in 2012-13 it slight declined and reached 22.92 per cent as compared to 2009-10. The average ratio was 23.47 per cent which was lower than industry average ratio. The above analysis indicated that the payment of dividend was regular in the company.

Centum Electronics Ltd.

Table no.13 clearly indicates that dividend pay-out ratio in CEL Company witnessed an increasing trend in first four years of study period. It was 8.5 per cent in 2003-04 and 23.34 per cent in 2006-07. In 2007-08 it was 12.97 per cent. In

2008-09, 2009 to 2010 and 2012-13 the company was not paid dividend. It ranged between 8.5 per cent in 2003-04 and 28.95 per cent in 2010-11. The average ratio was 11.901 per cent which was lower than industry average ratio.

MIRC Electronics Ltd.

Table no.13 the Dividend Payout Ratio of MEL Company recorded a fluctuating trend during the study period. The dividend pay-out ratio ranged between 88.63 per cent in 2009-10 and 34.96 per cent in 2007-08. The average ratio was 42.383 per cent which was higher than industry average ratio. The first eight years of study period the company had paid regular dividend but in last two years company had not paid any dividend it indicates that there was change in dividend policy of the company.

TVS Electronics Ltd.

Table no.13 clearly indicates that Dividend Payout Ratio of TEL Company witnessed an increasing trend in first four years of the study period. It was 40.73 per cent in 2003-04 and 83.48 per cent in 2006-07. In 2007-08 it was declined 16.17 per cent. The average ratio was 23.329 per cent which was lower than industry average ratio. The first six years of study period the company had paid regular dividend but in last four years company had not paid any dividend.

Blue Stare Ltd.

Table no.13 clearly indicates that Dividend Payout Ratio of BSL Company a decreasing trend in first seven years of the study period. It was 56.10 per cent in 2003-04 and 39.67 per cent in 2009-10, then after it was increasing 47.2 per cent in 2010-11 and 52.14 per cent in 2012-13. The average ratio was 42.45 per cent which was higher than industry average ratio. The first eight years of study period the company had paid regular dividend but in 2011-12 company had not paid any dividend.

F-Test (ANOVA):

Null Hypothesis: There is no any significance difference in dividend payout ratio of selected Electronics Companies in India.

Alternative Hypothesis: There is significance difference in dividend payout ratio of selected Electronics Companies in India.

For testing these hypothesis one way ANOVA test has been used as shown in table as below.

Table No. 14

F-Test (ANOVA) of Dividend Payout Ratio

Source of Variation	SS	d.f.	MS	F Value	F crit (5%)
Between Groups	7132.16	4	1783.041	4.2418	2.5787
Within Groups	18915.8	45	420.3511		
Total	26047.96	49			

The analysis showed the significance result. It can be seen from the table, that the calculated value of 'F' was found as 4.2418 while the table value of 'F' was 2.5787 at 5% level of significance. The calculated value of 'F' being greater than the table value 'F', the null hypothesis stood rejected and the alternative hypothesis accepted at 5% level of significance.

CHAPTER 6

SUMMERY, FINDINGS AND SUGGESTIONS

Chapter - 1 Conceptual Framework of Profitability

In this chapter analysis of profitability of Electronics units under study has been explained. Here concept of profit and profitability, factors affecting the profitability, Significance of profitability, techniques to measure profitability, concept of ratio analysis, purpose and types of ratios, importance of ratio analysis, benefits of ratio analysis, limitations of ratio analysis, Analysis of variance (f-test) has been discussed.

Chapter - 2 Overview of Electronics Industry

In the Indian context **N. Vittal** remarked "Electronics industry has witnessed significant growth during the sixth and seventh plan period with the growth rates being 25 and 35 percent respectively". Today most of the component and equipment including computers are entering our country from abroad due to the liberalized economic policy and these are essentially manufactured in these far eastern countries and the large market which has opened up in India in the field of electronics is now being fed by the production in those countries. As well as "After adopting new liberalized industrial policy-1991, many multinational companies are interested to take leading position over the Indian markets and customers.

Technological developments in electronics are international in nature and influence various sectors of economies of Nations as well as Human life, Cost structure, Quality and Productivity standards. Information Technology gets thrust from the mixture of communication, computers and entertainment areas. Development in the design and production of silicon chips permitted "Low cost, high speed and versatile information processing, control and storage capacity." Future developments in electronics sector may significantly change the lifecycle.

Chapter - 3 Research Methodology

The subject of the present study is "Analysis of Profitability of Electronics Industry in India" which covers the period of the last ten years 2003-04 to 2012-13. The study is based on secondary data published by the Electronics industry in their annual reports and accounts. The main objective of the present study is to measure profitability of concern industries and to find out the various factors which affect the profitability. Further to compare the performance of all the units researcher has used F-test (ANOVA) for the hypothesis testing.

Finally a survey of the exiting literature on the subject has been made and limitations of present study have been also shown.

CHAPTER - 4   SAMPLE PROFILE

This chapter includes the individual information of the each unit undertaken for the study. This chapter gives history, vision, mission, achievement, policy etc. of each co-operative dairy unit. Financial data from the period 2003-04 to 2012-13 is given. The data and the relevant information is obtained from the financial statements and annual reports of the company, various websites have been checked out and other publishing materials, journal, periodical have been referred out to collect the information about the units.

CHAPTER - 5   ANALYSIS OF PROFITABILITY

Finally, analysis of profitability with help of various profitability ratios based on financial statements has been given. Here various statements of hypothesis have been tested with help of statistical tools and techniques like mean, standard deviation, and F-test (ANOVA).

FINDINGS

❖ ANALYSIS OF PROFITABILITY

Profitability ratio shows the financial soundness of the electronics units. Management of the units always takes interest to know its operational efficiency. Here below the analysis and conclusion done of the profitability ratios.

Analysis of the profitability from the view point of Financial Management

1. OPERATING PROFIT RATIO:

Return on sales (operating margin) can be used both as a tool to analyze a single company's performance against its past performance, and to compare similar companies' performances against one another. The operating profit ratio of TEL was 0.07 percent in 2008-09, which was the lowest as compared to other Selected Electronics Units during the study period. BEL, CEL, MEL and TEL were recorded positive operating profit during the study period. BSL suffered losses during 2011-12. The operating profit ratio of CEL was 30.79 percent in 2003-04, which was the highest as compared to other Selected Electronics Units. The average operating profit ratio of the all selected electronics units was 9.989 percent.

On the basis of results obtained from 'F' test it may be concluded that the difference in operating profit ratio among the electronics units were significantce at 5 percent level of significance, because the calculated value of 'F' (17.3107) was greater than the table value 'F' (2.5787), the null hypothesis stood rejected and the alternative hypothesis accepted.

2. GROSS PROFIT RATIO:

This ratio expresses the relationship of gross profit to sales, in term of percentage. The gross profit ratio of TEL was 0.89 percent in 2012-13, which was the lowest as compared to other Selected Electronics Units during the study period. BEL was recorded positive gross profit during the study period. CEL, MEL, TEL and BSL suffered losses respectively during 2009-10 and 2012-13, 2011-13, 2007-10 and 2011-12. The gross profit ratio of BEL was 30.73 percent in 2003-04, which was the highest as compared to other Selected Electronics Units. The average gross profit ratio of the all selected electronics units was 8.056 percent.

On the basis of results obtained from 'F' test it may be concluded that the difference in gross profit ratio among the electronics units were significance at 5 percent level of significance, because the calculated value of 'F' (10.8517) was greater than the table value 'F' (2.5787), the null hypothesis stood rejected and the alternative hypothesis accepted.

3. RETURN ON CAPITAL EMPLOYED

The return on capital employed of TEL was 0.06 percent in 2008-09, which was the lowest as compared to other selected electronics units during the study period. BEL and TEL were recorded positive return on capital employed during the study period. CEL, MEL and BSL suffered losses respectively during 2012-13, 2011-13 and 2011-12. The return on capital employed of BSL was 69.82 percent in 2007-08, which was the highest as compared to other Selected Electronics Units. The average return on capital employed of the all selected Electronics units was 20.04 percent.

On the basis of results obtained from 'F' test it may be concluded that the difference in return on capital employed ratio among the electronics units were significance at 5 percent level of significance, because the calculated value of 'F' (7.8285) being greater than the table value 'F' (2.5787), the null hypothesis stood rejected and the alternative hypothesis accepted.

Analysis of the profitability from the view point of Shareholder's:

1. NET PROFIT RATIO:

Net profit ratio establishes relationship between net profit and sales. It also indicates management's efficiency in manufacturing, administering and selling the products. The net profit ratio of MEL was 0.54 percent in 2008-09, which was the lowest as compared to other Selected Electronics Units during the study period. BEL was recorded positive net profit during the study period. CEL, MEL, TEL and BSL suffered losses respectively during 2009-10 and 2012-13, 2011-13, 2008-10 and 2012-13 and 2011-12. The net profit ratio of CEL was 29.78 percent in 2004-05, which was the highest as compared to other Selected Electronics Units. The average net profit ratio of the all selected electronics units was 5.974 percent.

On the basis of results obtained from 'F' test it may be concluded that the difference in net profit ratio among the electronics units were significance at 5 percent level of significance, because the calculated value of 'F' (12.2577) was greater than the table value 'F' (2.5787), the null hypothesis stood rejected and the alternative hypothesis accepted.

2. RETURN ON NET WORTH / SHAREHOLDERS EQUITY:

One of the objectives of operating a company is to seek benefit of its shareholders. The return on net worth of CEL was 1.14 percent in 2008-09, which was the lowest as compared to other selected electronics units during the study period. BEL was recorded positive return on net worth during the study period. CEL, MEL, TEL and BSL suffered losses respectively during 2009-10 and 2012-13, 2011-13, 2008-10 and 2012-13 and 2011-12. The return on net worth of BSL was 66.32 percent in 2007-08, which was the highest as compared to other Selected Electronics Units. The average return on net worth of the all selected Electronics units was 15.021 percent.

On the basis of results obtained from 'F' test it may be concluded that the difference in return on net worth ratio among the electronics units were significance at 5 percent level of significance, because the calculated value of 'F' (4.8504) being greater than the table value 'F' (2.5787), the null hypothesis stood rejected and the alternative hypothesis accepted.

3. EARING PER SHARE

The earning per share of CEL was Rs. 0.50 in 2008-09, which was the lowest as compared to other Selected Electronics Units during the study period. BEL was recorded positive earnings per share during the study period. CEL, MEL, TEL and BSL suffered losses respectively during 2009-10 and 2012-13, 2011-13, 2008-10 and 2012-13 and 2011-12. The earning per share of BEL was Rs. 113.90 in 2012-13, which was the highest as compared to other selected electronics units. The average earning per share of the all selected electronics units was Rs. 22.282.

On the basis of results obtained from 'F' test it may be concluded that the difference in earning per share among the electronics units were significance at 5 percent level of significance, because the calculated value of 'F' (108.0646) being greater than the table value 'F' (2.5787), the null hypothesis stood rejected and the alternative hypothesis accepted.

4. DIVIDEND PAYOUT RATIO:

The dividend payout ratio of CEL was 8.5 in 2003-04, which was the lowest as compared to other Selected Electronics Units during the study period. The dividend did not declare in CEL, MEL, TEL and BSL respectively during in 2008 to 2010 and 2012-13, 2011 to 13, 2008 to 2013 and 2011-12 due to net loss. The dividend payout ratio of MEL was 88.63 in 2009-10, which was the highest as compared to other selected electronics units. The average dividend payout ratio of the all selected electronics units was 28.7086 percent.

On the basis of results obtained from 'F' test it may be concluded that the difference in earning per share among the electronics units were significance at 5 percent level of significance, because the calculated value of 'F' (108.0646) being greater than the table value 'F' (2.5787), the null hypothesis stood rejected and the alternative hypothesis accepted.

Conclusion:

Analysis of profitability above three ratios under the study by all selected Electronics Companies; the results obtained from 'F' test (ANOVA) may be concluded that there is significance difference between profitability in all ratios of selected electronics companies in India.

SUGGESTIONS

❖ The average Operating Profit Ratio of TVS Electronics Ltd was lowest as compared to other Selected Electronics Companies. The average Operating Profit Ratio of Bharat Electronics Ltd was highest as compared to other Selected Electronics Companies. It indicates that the earning capacity of Bharat Electronics Ltd was higher as compared to other Selected Electronics

Companies. Therefore, higher the ratio, the better would be the operational efficiency of the firm.

❖ The average Gross Profit Ratio of TVS Electronics Ltd was lowest as compared to other Selected Electronics Companies. The average Gross Profit Ratio of Bharat Electronics Ltd was highest as compared to other Selected Electronics Companies. The earning capacity of Bharat Electronics Ltd was higher as compared to other Selected Electronics Companies. A high gross profit ratio suggests that the cost of production was relatively low and a low ratio suggest that the cost of production was not under control.

❖ The average Net Profit Ratio of TVS Electronics Ltd was lowest as compared to other Selected Electronics Companies. The average Net Profit Ratio of Bharat Electronics Ltd. was highest as compared to other Selected Electronics Companies. It indicates that the earning capacity of Bharat Electronics Ltd was higher as compared to other Selected Electronics Companies. Therefore, other Selected Electronics Companies should to take steps for better sales realization and reduction of the cost of production.

❖ The average Return on Capital Employed Profit Ratio of TVS Electronics Ltd was lowest as compared to other Selected Electronics Companies. The average Return on Capital Employed Profit Ratio of Blue Star Ltd was highest as compared to other Selected Electronics Companies.

❖ The average Dividend Payout Ratio of Centum Electronics Ltd was lowest as compared to other Selected Electronics Companies. The average Dividend Payout Ratio of Blue Star Ltd was highest as compared to other Selected Electronics Companies. The payout ratio and the retained earnings ratio are indicators of the amount of earning that have been ploughed back in the business, lower the payout ratio, higher will be the amount of earning ploughed back in the business.

❖ The average Earning Per Share Ratio of TVS Electronics Ltd was lowest as compared to other Selected Electronics Companies. The average Earning Per Share Ratio of Bharat Electronics Ltd was highest as compared to other Selected Electronics Companies. EPS is a widely used ratio. In general higher the figure better it is and vice versa ,while interpreting this ratio it must be seen whether there was any increase in equity share holders fund as a result of retained earning without any change in number of outstanding shares.

BIBLIOGRAPHY

BOOKS:

1. Cherunilam Francis (1989), Industrial Economics: Indian perspective, Himalaya Publishing House, Bombay , p.483

2. Nagrajan Vittal (1991), Indian Electronics Industry and the new policy paradigm, EFY, New Delhi, November, p.23-26.

3. Ahuja Shobha, Electronics sector and liberalization, the economic times, Ahmedabad, 7th December 1996, p.5

4. The Institution of Radio Engineers(IRF) Proceedings, vol.38 , 1950

5. Matriculation Physics and Chemistry, Robert Macle House and Co. Ltd., Glasgow, p.489

6. Young E. C. (1982), The new penguin dictionary of electronics, penguin books ltd. Middlesex, p.616

7. Grob Bernard (1988), Basic Electronic Communication, McGraw Hill, Kogakusha, p.3

8. Shrader R. L. (1988), Electronics Communication, McGraw Book Company, New York , p.698

9. Kaushik D. N. (1987), Ham Radio, Harshal Publications, Ahmedabad, p.18

10. Zherebtsov I. (1988), Basic Electronics, Mir Publicashers, Moscow, p.11

11. Zherebtsov I.(1988), Basic Electronics, Op. Cit., p.12

12. Shore B. H. (1970), The new Electronics, McGraw HillBook Company, New York, p.13

13. Bhagrava N. N., Kulsherstha D. C. & Gupta S. C. (1984), Basic Electronics and Linear Circuits, Tata McGraw Hill Publishing Co. Ltd., New Delhi, p.4

14. Bhunia C. T. (May 1992), Molecular Electronics and Chemical Computer Technology, EFY, New Delhi, p.90

15. Singer H. W., Hatti Neelambar and Tandon Rameshwer (1988), Technology Transfer by Multinationals, Ashish Publishing House, New Delhi, Vol. 1, p.32

16. Minz S. M. & Arora R. K., Capital Goods for electronics industry in India, Instruments Electronics & Developments (IED), October 1996, Mumbai, p.14

17. Government of India, Annual Report 1996-97, Dept. of Electronics New Delhi, p.91

18. Consumer Electronic, Expert, Hunter Publishing Ltd., Illinois, Nov., Dec. 1992, p.8

19. Grob Bernard, Op. cit, p.6

20. Krishnamurthy T. G., Electro medical Industry current status and future trends, EFY, New Delhi, June 1985, p.28

21. Prasad Mahesh, Electronics Industry in India, EFY, New Delhi, September 1992, p.99

22. Nazareth J. and Dharmadhikari V., Electronics and Science Interventions, EFY, New Delhi, May 1995 p.54

23. Pithadia V. H., Fiber Optics : Status in India, Technical research paper was presented at 14th Gujarat science Congress at Palitana on 10-11th Oct. 1998, p.4

24. Government of India, Annual Report 1995-96, Dept. of electronics, New Delhi, p.31

25. Noel J.W., The future direction of Instrumentations, IED, Mumbai, January 1997, p.22

26. Kothari C. R. (1997), Research Methodology: Method & Techniques, 2nd Edition, Published by Wishwa Prakashan, New Delhi, p.2.

27. Cherunilam Francis (1989), Industrial Economics: Indian perspective, Published by Himalaya Publishing House, Bombay, p.483.

28. Michael V. P. (1985), Research Methodology in Management, Published by Himalayan Publishing House, Bombay, p.107.

29. Claire Selitiz (1962), Research Methodology in Social Sciences, Op Cit, p.50.

30. Powal L.S. and Kumar Vinod, Financial Statements Analysis and Prediction of Future of Return: A case study of engineering industry, Charted Accountant, 11th May 1998, p.988.

31. Batty J. (1966), Management Accountancy, Orient Longmans, New Delhi, p.394.

32. Gulerian R. C., Statistic for Decision Making, W. B. Saunders Company, Philadelphia, p.29-30.

33. Donald L. Harnett and Murphy James L., Introductory Statistical Analysis, p.376.

34. Levin Richard I. (1979), Statistics for Management, Prentice Hall of India Pvt. Ltd., New Delhi.

35. Braveman J. D. (1979), Fundamentals of Business Statistic, Academic Press, New York.

36. Bradely James V. (1968), Distribution frees Statistical Tests, Englewood Clifts, Prentice Hall Inc., New Jersey.

37. Stevenson W. J. (1978), Business Statistics, Harper and Row, New York.

38. Parmar. S. J.: Financial Efficiency, Raj Book Enterprises, Jaipur, India, p.39.

39. Gupta L. N.: Profitability in Public Sector, Oxford & IBH Publishing, New Delhi, 1977, p. 23.

40. Howard, Bion B., Upton and Miller: Introduction to Business Finance, McGraw - Hill Book Co., New York, International Edition, P.147.

41.   Weston, J. F. and Brigham E. F.: Essentials of Managerial Finance, Holt, Rinehart and Winston, Inc., New York, Forth Edition, P.47.

42.   R.S. Kulshretha: Profitability in India's steel industry during 1960-70.

43.   Pillai R. S. N. & Bagavathi: Management Accounting, 9th Edition, Published by Sultanchand & Companies Ltd, New Delhi -2009, p . 26-48.

44.   C.M. Chaudhary: Research Methodology, RSBA Publishers, Jaipur, 1999, p. 197.

45.   A. Tom Neslon: management Accounting, Macmillan, New York, 1970, p.238.

46.   I. M. Pandey: Financial Management, Vikas Publishing House Pvt. Ltd., New Delhi, 2002.

47.   S. C. Kuchhal: Financial Management – An Analytical and Conceptual Approach, Chaitanya Publishing House, Allahabad, 1993.

48.   M. Y. Khan & P. K. Jain: Financial Management – Text and Problems, Tata McGraw – Hill Publishing Company Limited, New Delhi, 2003.

JOURNALS, MAGAZINES, ARTICLES & PERIODICALS:

1. The National Manufacturing Competitiveness Council (2006)

2. Ministry of Commerce and Industry (2008)

3. National Council for Applied Economic Research (August 2007)

4. Ministry of Heavy Industries and Public Enterprises (2004 to 2008)

5. Ministry of Commerce and Industry (2003 to 2008)

6. Global Electronics Industry (2008-13)

7. Global Value Chains in the Electronics Industry, the world bank, September 2010

8. ELCINA, Dep. of Information Technology Ministry of Communications & Information Technology Govt. of India (2007 to 14)

9. Government of India Various Annual Reports, Dept. of Electronics, New Delhi (1991 to 2012)

10. Dept. of Information Technology Annual Report (2005 to 2013)

NEWS PAPERS:

1. The Financial Express (2007, 2008)
2. The Hindu Business Line (2007, 2008)

WEBSITE:

www.capitalline.com

www.economicstimes.com

www.blonnet.com

www.moneycntrol.com

www.reportgallery.com

www.annualreportservice.com

www.nse-india.com

www.sec.gov

www.business-standard.com

www.ingramcontent.com/pod-product-compliance
Lightning Source LLC
Chambersburg PA
CBHW080809180526
45168CB00006B/2375